TIME

100 Ideas That Changed the World

History's Greatest Breakthroughs,
Inventions, and Theories

FORWARD PROGRESS *In March 1965, Dr. Martin Luther King Jr. leads
a historic voting-rights march from Selma to Montgomery, Ala.*

TIME

MANAGING EDITOR Richard Stengel
ART DIRECTOR D.W. Pine
EDITORIAL DIRECTOR, TIME BOOKS Stephen Koepp

100 Ideas That Changed the World

History's Greatest Breakthroughs, Inventions, and Theories

EDITOR/WRITER Richard Lacayo
DESIGNER Sharon Okamoto
PICTURE EDITOR Dot McMahon
RESEARCHERS Kathleen Adams, Barbara Burke, and Lisa McLaughlin
EDITORIAL PRODUCTION Lionel P. Vargas

TIME HOME ENTERTAINMENT
PUBLISHER Richard Fraiman
GENERAL MANAGER Steven Sandonato
EXECUTIVE DIRECTOR, MARKETING SERVICES Carol Pittard
DIRECTOR, RETAIL & SPECIAL SALES Tom Mifsud
DIRECTOR, NEW PRODUCT DEVELOPMENT Peter Harper
DIRECTOR, BOOKAZINE DEVELOPMENT & MARKETING Laura Adam
PUBLISHING DIRECTOR, BRAND MARKETING Joy Butts
ASSISTANT GENERAL COUNSEL Helen Wan
BOOK PRODUCTION MANAGER Suzanne Janso
DESIGN & PREPRESS MANAGER Anne-Michelle Gallero
BRAND MANAGER Michela Wilde

SPECIAL THANKS TO:
Christine Austin, Jeremy Biloon, Glenn Buonocore, Jim Childs, Susan Chodakiewicz,
Rose Cirrincione, Brian Fellows, Jacqueline Fitzgerald, Carrie Frazier, Lauren Hall,
Malena Jones, Brynn Joyce, Mona Li, Robert Marasco, Kimberly Marshall,
Amy Migliaccio, Dave Rozzelle, Ilene Schreider, Adriana Tierno, Alex Voznesenskiy,
Vanessa Wu, Time Imaging

Published by TIME Books, an imprint of Time Home Entertainment Inc.
135 West 50th St., New York, NY 10020

ISBN 13: 978-1-60320-170-4 ISBN 10: 1-60320-170-X
Library of Congress Control Number: 2010941154

We welcome your comments and suggestions about TIME Books. Please write to us at:
TIME Books, Attention: Book Editors, PO Box 11016, Des Moines, IA 50336-1016

If you would like to order any of our hardcover Collector's Edition books,
please call us at 1-800-327-6388.
Monday–Friday, 7 a.m.–8 p.m., or Saturday, 7 a.m.–6 p.m., Central Time

THE MIND OF THE CENTURY *Albert Einstein
lecturing at the College de France in Paris in 1922,
one year after being awarded the Nobel Prize in
Physics for his groundbreaking theoretical work*

Contents

ANCIENT SAGE *The serene face of the Daibutsu, the Great Buddha of Kamakura, a 13th-century monumental bronze statue in Kamakura, Japan*

One Hundred Crucial Products of the Tireless Human Mind

Ideas are funny things. Invisible and weightless, they have no material substance, yet they have the power to change the course of history. Or as the French writer Victor Hugo put it: "One can resist invading armies; one cannot resist an invasion of ideas."

The fact is, in an undertaking as complex as the whole of human history, there are many more than 100 essential ideas. Where, you may ask, in the book we offer here, are agriculture, Brahma, and the telephone? What happened to Baruch Spinoza, David Hume, and John Dewey? Why no second law of thermodynamics, quantum mechanics, and dark matter? And while we're at it, what about the wheel?

All of those were on the list of candidates this project began with. But after much thought—something that seemed appropriate for a book about ideas—the 100 we settled upon stood out to us in part because taken together they demonstrate the many different things an idea can be. Those would include centuries-in-the-making developments like the alphabet and codified law; schools of thought like stoicism and existentialism; cultural watersheds that took place on many fronts, like humanism and romanticism; individual intellectual breakthroughs like those of Descartes or Darwin; and crucial inventions like photography and computers. And while the ideas under discussion in this book are not the only ones that shaped the course of human affairs, we're confident they rank among the most important.

As a pioneer of science fiction, the British novelist H.G. Wells was especially attuned to the allure of new modes of thought. This is why he could say that "Human history is, in essence, a history of ideas." We would agree. The ideas in this book didn't merely change history. They are the very substance of history itself. —*The Editors*

THE THINKER *A copy of Auguste Rodin's famous bronze, here on temporary display in Barcelona*

6

OLD GLORY *Columns outside the Theater of Marcellus in Rome, which was built in the first century B.C.*

Ancient World

ANIMAL MAGNETISM *In the Lascaux Caves in southwestern France, a prehistoric painting shows horses and a bull.*

Prehistoric Man Imagines a World Inhabited by Spirits

1 "The world is alive." You might say that was the central tenet of the earliest form of religion, one that we generally call "animism." It's a term that was coined in 1871 by pioneering British anthropologist Edward Burnett Tylor. He used it to describe what he had concluded was one of the first spiritual intuitions, the belief among prehistoric people that all things, both living and inanimate, are inhabited by spirit. In the animist worldview, not just humans, but animals and plants, rivers and mountains, even stones—all contain what might be called a soul. In his book *Primitive Culture*, Tylor explained that primitive peoples regarded this "ghost-soul," when it inhabited a person, as "the cause of life and thought in the individual it animates."

For primitive man, it was the desires and moods of the animating spirits that explained many of the phenomena of the natural world, like what they believed to be the anger of thunder clouds. Sometimes humans could summon or appease those spirits through the use of ritual and magic, the mysterious specialties of the tribal figures called shamans.

Tylor decided that the animist worldview eventually evolved into polytheism. The individual spirit residing in each river, for instance, might eventually be understood as part of a collective of river gods. But even in the modern world there are cultures that retain an animist outlook. Among tribal communities of Africa and the Brazilian rainforest, and among some of the native peoples of the U.S. and Canada, belief in a multitude of spirits remains a foundation of their religion. And the spirit of animism also lives on in the concept of the human soul developed by many faiths, including Hinduism, Buddhism, Christianity, and Islam.

A Multitude of Gods Give Way to One God Almighty

2 In the societies of the ancient world, there were numerous gods and goddesses. River gods, sky gods, local deities, animal-headed demon gods—in a survey at the dawn of the third millennium B.C., scribes in Mesopotamia counted nearly 2,000 deities among the various city-states. But in Egypt in the 14th century B.C., Pharaoh Amenhotep IV made a radical attempt to introduce monotheism. His god was Aten, the life-giving disc of the sun—and such was his devotion to this god that around 1346 B.C., early in his reign, Amenhotep abandoned his dynastic name and christened himself Akhenaten—"Servant of Aten." And he served Aten well. He closed the old state temples and directed most religious funds to Aten's priests. He had the plural word "gods" erased from some religious texts and dissolved the priesthoods of the other deities. He founded a great city, Akhetaten, that was dedicated to Aten, and he moved the capital there.

But Akhenaten's new religion proved too alien to his people to survive his death, which occurred some 17 years into his reign. Soon after becoming pharaoh, his son Tutankhaten renounced Aten and changed his name to Tutankhamun–a nod to the god Amun who had been one of the chief Egyptian deities before the short-lived supremacy of Aten. "King Tut" even went on to abandon his father's new city.

FATHER FIGURE *On the ceiling of the Sistine Chapel in Rome, Michelangelo depicts God creating the sun, moon, and planets.*

So it fell to the tribes of Israel to become the first people to embrace decisively the worship of a single God. They too were originally polytheists, and the Hebrew Bible, what Christians call the Old Testament, is full of stories of occasional backsliding among them, as with their worship of the golden calf. The beginning of their commitment to one God begins very early in the Bible, however, with the story of Abraham. It may be no more than a story. Apart from Scripture, there appears to be no evidence that he was a genuine historical figure. But he is regarded as a patriarch by three great religions, Judaism, Christianity, and Islam, and he symbolizes their core commitment to one Lord.

We first encounter Abraham in the Book of Genesis, where he is presented to us as a member of a family that sold idols but who turns away from polytheism when the Lord appears to him and they make a covenant. Abraham will be the father of a great nation, the Lord promises; in return, Abraham must circumcise himself as a sign of his devotion to his single Lord.

If Abraham did live, historians believe it would have been between 2100 B.C. and 1500 B.C., hundreds of years before the date that most of them assign to Judaism's origins. Fact or fable, he represents a revolution in thought, the decisive turning away from polytheism to the belief in one all-powerful God.

The World of Mathematical Form Takes Shape

3 | The abstract realm of mathematics began on very solid ground—in fact, literal ground. In ancient Egypt, the Nile river flooded its banks every year. When the waters retreated, they left behind deposits of fertile soil that made agriculture possible in the plains on both sides of the river. But the floodwaters also washed away boundary markers that established property lines around planting fields. For that reason surveyors would be sent out annually by the pharaoh to reset the markers, using knotted ropes to measure plots and mark right angles. In time they learned to estimate the plots by dividing them into rectangles and triangles. In this way they invented geometry, the earliest form of mathematics.

Other cultures of the ancient world, in Babylon and the Indus valley, would also develop geometric formulas. But geometry's great leap forward would come with the Greeks, who coined the term by combining their words for "Earth"—*geo*—and "to measure"—*metros*. The key figure in Greek mathematics was Euclid (c. 325–265 B.C.), whose mighty treatise, *The Elements*, is the first known attempt to make geometry into a system.

Geometry introduced the idea of ideal forms existing outside the physical world. It opened vistas onto forms and ratios so beautiful they seemed to offer a look into the mind of God. Plato held that God is a geometer. The Greek mathematician Pythagoras and his followers formed a religious brotherhood that venerated the triangle. They also discovered something they called the golden ratio, a figure they achieved by dividing a line in two so that the ratio of the small part to the large part is the same as the ratio of the large part to the whole. This most satisfying of geometric relationships also fascinated many thinkers of the Renaissance, who found it everywhere in art and nature. In his 1509 treatise, *De divina proportione*, Luca Paccioli would even claim to find correspondences between the ratio and characteristics of the Supreme Being. Geometry, which began on the ground, reached ultimately toward heaven.

VISIONS OF THE NEXT WORLD *Top right, the jackal-headed Egyptian god Anubis attends to the mummy of the artisan Sennedjem; above, a painted Etruscan terra cotta plaque shows Hercules rescuing Alcestis, the noble wife of King Admetus, from Hades; at top, a detail from* The Garden of Earthly Delights, *a triptych that Dutch artist Hieronymus Bosch painted around 1500, shows the damned suffering the torments of hell.*

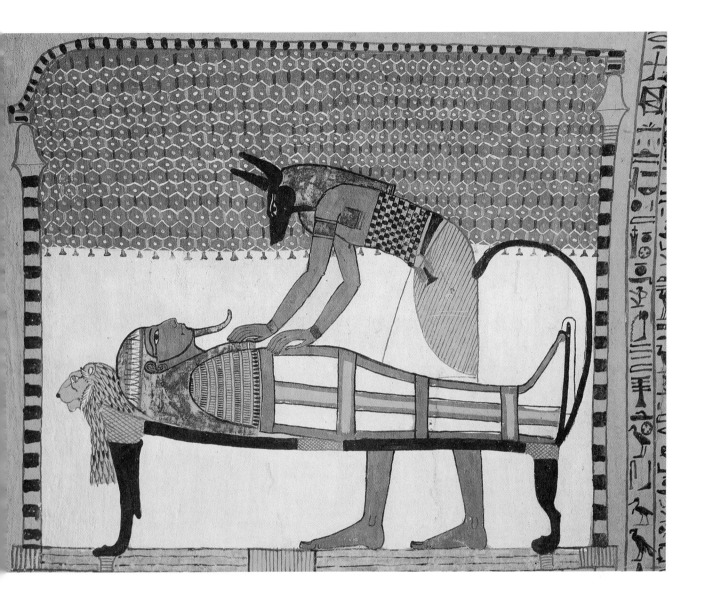

Mankind Envisions Life After Death

The Great Pyramid of Giza, one of the oldest surviving monumental structures, is a testament to one of humankind's most enduring and compelling ideas: the afterlife. There is virtually no civilization that hasn't developed some notion of life after death. In the absence of anything that could be called reliable physical evidence, men and women of every era and culture have reached for a picture of life's journey in which the grave is merely an entryway to a new stage, not a final destination.

For the Egyptians, the afterlife was a journey, in the company of the jackal-headed god Anubis, to the soul's final judgment. The Greeks imagined an underworld ruled by Hades, which souls entered by crossing the river Styx with the boatman Charon. Both Hinduism and Buddhism believe the soul is reborn after death, sometimes in another human form, sometimes in a lower form. Heaven is effectively an escape from that cycle of rebirth, which both religions offer ways to achieve, and a merger with the ultimate reality.

Islam has a notion of both heaven and hell. So, too, Christianity, which would add a third compartment to the edifice of the afterlife. In the seventh century, Pope Gregory would elaborate the doctrine of purgatory, which by the 13th century would be further refined into the idea of a sort of holding pen for souls who had hope of eventually entering heaven but still needed to expiate the guilt of minor sins. In time that doctrine would provide a controversial revenue stream for the Church, which took to selling "indulgences" to the living intended to reduce the time their souls would spend in purgatory.

THE LONG ARM OF THE LAW *At the top of the stele on which his Code is inscribed, the Babylonian King Hammurabi appears seated on his throne.*

King Hammurabi Lays Down the Law

5 Reviled and admired, envied and feared, ancient Babylon—the remains of which lie some 50 miles (80 km) south of Baghdad—has for centuries been shrouded in myth. Despite its description by Greek historians as a center of political power, lingering fables tend to overshadow any sense of what the city was actually like. "Everyone knows the name and the legends of Babylon," Francis Joannès, a professor of ancient history at the Sorbonne, told *Time* in 2008. "But what people don't necessarily know is its reality." Yet nothing could be more real than the magnificent Code of Hammurabi stele, a seven-foot-high (2 m) column of basalt upon which Babylon's king inscribed 282 codified laws and punishments in cuneiform, the Babylonian script that predates hieroglyphs. This ancient tablet is one of the earliest known written records of the laws that give order and shape to human society, and of those early examples it is by far the most complex.

Ruling in the early 18th century B.C., Hammurabi, the sixth king of Babylon, used an aggressive military policy to conquer rival city-states and to establish Babylon as Mesopotamia's political heart, a status it would retain until 539 B.C. But Hammurabi was concerned about more than expansion, as reflected by the laws carved upon the stele. Although its prescriptions sound extreme today ("If a man commits a robbery and is caught, that man will be killed"), they helped Hammurabi craft his image as a just ruler. The stele was displayed publicly, so no citizen, regardless of status, could plead ignorance of its laws.

The stele bearing Hammurabi's Code was discovered by French archaeologists in 1901 in Iran's Khuzestan province, where it had been carried as plunder in the 12th century B.C. It is a reminder that kings and kingdoms may perish, but society's need for laws is eternal.

OLD LETTERS *Clockwise from left, Sumerian cuneiform inscribed across a circular clay tablet from around 1980 B.C.; a dedication stone for a street in ancient Carthage written in the Phoenician alphabet; Chinese calligraphy in the fourth-century* Letter Written on a Snowy Day

The Alphabet Emerges

6 Scholars cannot tell us when humans first began to speak distinct languages, but they are more certain about the first appearance of written communication in the form of the alphabet. There is a dizzying array of alphabets, of course. The Chinese began using pictograms, pictures standing for words, around 5000 B.C. Egypt was another home of early writing; its hieroglyphs were a combination of characters and pictograms. The oldest-known date from 3400 to about 3200 B.C.

Unlike hieroglyphics, Chinese pictograms have survived into the present as a living system. So have Hebrew, Greek, and Arabic letters, as well as the Persian alphabet derived from Arabic and the related Urdu alphabet of Pakistan. The Cyrillic alphabet, a descendant of the Greek, is used today by Russians and other Slavic peoples. Then there's the Korean alphabet, and the Hindi, used in India and elsewhere.

But the single most widely used modern system of letters is the Latin alphabet, the one employed for English and the other languages of the Western world. It ultimately derives from a system that began in ancient Sumer, a Mesopotamian civilization that sometime before 3400 B.C. developed cuneiform, a pictographic system made of wedge-shaped marks pressed with the edge of a stylus into clay tablets. But the "letters" of the early cuneiform system often identified whole words or ideas, not sounds like a modern alphabet. The Phoenicians took that final step. A commercial people based in the region that is now Lebanon, they adapted cuneiform by reducing the number of pictographs until its symbols finally emerged as letters. Sometime around 1000 B.C., the Phoenicians came in contact with the ancient Greeks, who absorbed and adapted the Phoenician alphabet and gave it a name, drawn from the first two letters of the Greek alphabet—alpha and beta. The Greeks passed it to the Etruscans, who handed it on to the Romans, who delivered it to the rest of us.

CLOCKWISE FROM LEFT: THE GRANGER COLLECTION; ERICH LESSING/ART RESOURCE; LEE & LEE COMMUNICATIONS/ART RESOURCE

15

The Week Gets Seven Days

7 So accustomed are we to the seven-day week that it probably never occurs to most people that in the past some cultures observed a very different calendar. The ancient Egyptians had a 10-day week. So did the Chinese. The idea for a seven-day week originated with the ancient Babylonians. They worshipped the sun and the moon as gods. They also recognized that most of the stars seemed fixed in the same position night after night, but that five of them moved back and forth throughout the year. We know now that those moving "stars" are actually planets. The Babylonians knew only that they were powerful and important, so they identified each of them with one of their gods or goddesses. And they gave to each of the seven days of their week the names of one of the seven deities connected to the sun, the moon, and the five planets.

The Babylonian seven-day system was eventually taken on by the Romans, who operated for a long time with an eight-day week as part of a calendar that continually fell out of alignment with the actual solar year. But after the Romans adopted the Julian calendar in the first century A.D., the seven-day week gradually came into use, until it was officially adopted by the Emperor Constantine in 321 A.D. The Romans simply substituted the names of their own gods for the Babylonian deities.

The English-language names for each day are derived from a combination of Roman and Norse gods. Sunday and Monday, of course, are for the sun and the moon. But Tuesday derives from Tyr, the Norse god of war, and Wednesday from Odin, sometimes spelled Wodin, the chief god of the Norse pantheon. Thursday is for Thor, the god of thunder, and Friday for Freya, who was Odin's wife. Saturday refers to a Roman deity again—Saturn, god of agriculture and the harvest.

After the Roman Empire fell, when the Catholic Church emerged as the chief institution of the Western world, it retained the seven-day week, which neatly corresponded to the biblical account of God creating the universe in six days—and resting on the seventh.

ROUNDUP *A weekly calendar appears on the left of this 18th-century German card that uses revolving paper disks to also provide information about zodiac signs, feast days, and phases of the moon.*

HARD JUDGMENT *A potsherd used as a ballot in the practice of "ostracism," in which Athenians could vote to banish other citizens.*

People Learn to Rule Themselves

8 Almost everywhere in the ancient world, men and women were ruled by emperors, kings, and pharaohs. The exception was Greece, where many of the city-states adopted a form of government they called *demokratia*, from the Greek *demos*, meaning "the people," and *kratis*, "rule." Like so much else in Greece, democracy achieved its most highly developed form in Athens. Around the end of the sixth century B.C., the Athenians established a system in which citizens were chosen by lot to fill government offices and all citizens were invited to debate in the assembly. Though women, slaves, and males under 20 were excluded, no previous form of government had ever recognized the right of so many people to take part in decision-making.

The Romans later adapted the Greek forms to create a republic, in which citizens voted for senators, consuls, and tribunes. But with the fall of Rome, representative government, already weakened by Rome's transition from republic to empire, went into a long retreat. It would make a lasting return to the conversation in England, especially in the 17th century, in the struggles by the British Parliament to restrain the powers of the king and the widening debate over abolishing property qualifications for the vote.

The American and French revolutions would prove to be the turning point. Today most of the world's people live under an elected government, however imperfect. Democracy can be an exasperating, messy system—or as Winston Churchill called it, "the worst form of government—except for all those other forms that have been tried from time to time."

An Enlightened Asian Seeker
Founds an Enduring Philosophy

9 In the beginning, it is said, the Buddha found enlightenment beneath the bodhi tree, near what is now Nepal.
Siddhartha Gautama was a pampered prince born around
563 B.C. who frustrated his father's efforts to shield him from the
sights of suffering and death, became a wandering holy man, and
eventually formulated the Four Noble Truths that unite all Bud-
dhists today. Life, declared the Buddha, or "Enlightened One," is full
of suffering. Most of that suffering, including the fear of death, can
be traced to "desire," the mind's habit of seeing everything through
the prism of the self and its well-being. Yet this craving can be
transcended, leading to peace and eventually to an exalted state of
full enlightenment called Nirvana. The means to reach Nirvana lies
in the Eightfold Path of proper views, resolve, speech, action,
livelihood, effort, mindfulness, and concentration.

The Truths dovetailed with India's ancient Hindu scheme of
reincarnation: Every human is reborn again and again, in an endless
and wearying cycle called samsara, each life affected by the good
and bad deeds performed in previous existences, according to a
system called karma. The attainment of Nirvana allows us finally to
step away from this cycle and enter into oneness with the cosmos,
and meditation is the best way to reach enlightenment.

The Buddha posited no creator God. His Truths are so distinct
from the primary concerns of other faiths that some Western ob-
servers regard Buddhism as a philosophy or even a psychology. Yet
because it puts so little emphasis on specific doctrines, and because
Buddha himself is regarded as a sage rather than a god, Buddhism
has proved highly malleable; its various branches have been adapted
to suit cultures far from Asia. Ironically, Buddhism is now little
practiced in the land of its birth, India. But around the globe, some
325 million followers continue to meditate, seeking to share with
Buddha the enlightenment he found beneath the bodhi tree.

THE SERENE ONE *A 14th-century Tibetan fabric painting depicts the Buddha. His
followers do not regard him as a god but as a human who achieved enlightenment,
the condition that permits escape from the cycle of rebirth.*

A Chinese Sage Creates a Guide for Personal Conduct

10 "Forget injuries; never forget kindnesses."
"What the superior man seeks is in himself; what the small man seeks is in others."
"Have no friends not equal to yourself."

So spoke the Chinese philosopher K'ung-Tze (551–478 B.C.), better known to Westerners by his Latinized name, Confucius. For a while he was an adviser to one of the warring chieftains of his day, before retiring to become master to a circle of students. Taken together, his teachings form a complex system of social, political, moral, and religious ideas, one that provided for millennia a guide for both individual conduct and the organization of society in China and throughout East Asia. Like Christ and Socrates, Confucius left behind no writings of his own. As with them, we know of his teachings through the records of his disciples. The most important are collected in the *Analects*, a book of his maxims interspersed with anecdotes and bits of conversation.

Confucius believed that all people live within limits established by Heaven, which for him meant both a Supreme Being and the fixed cycles of nature. All the same, they are responsible for their actions and how they treat others—and Heaven depends upon them to carry out its good intentions. His rules for the virtuous life were simple: to love others, to honor one's parents, to do things because they are right and not merely to win advantage. He put heavy emphasis on rituals and on setting a good example as a means to ensure the spread of righteousness.

More than a century after Confucius died, his ideas were developed further by the philosopher Mencius, and in the second century B.C. were adopted in that systematized version as the official doctrine of the Han dynasty. This marked the beginning of their institutionalization as China's "state religion." A few centuries later, the Tang dynasty made the Confucian classics the basis of the famous civil service exams that produced the class of magistrates, called mandarins, who would be the administrators of the Chinese empire. For centuries they would wield extraordinary power throughout China —exercised in accordance with the precepts of the master.

ROVING MASTER *A statue of Confucius in Vietnam's Ho Chi Minh City. From China, Confucian ideas spread widely throughout East Asia.*

LEADING FOLLOWER *Second-century Roman Emperor Marcus Aurelius, author of* Meditations, *a Stoic classic*

The Stoics Urge a Life of "Stoical" Forbearance

11 In roughly the same years that comfort-seeking Epicureanism first flourished, the fourth century B.C., a school of philosophy emerged in Athens that preached a very different view of life. Zeno and his followers, the first Stoics, believed that God permeated the universe and also that God was absolute reason. This led them to conclude that the universe was governed by laws of cause and effect, which in turn meant that there was no true free will. Therefore the highest wisdom, or virtue, as they called it, was to recognize necessity and not to resist it, to "live in agreement with nature." In that pursuit, passions and appetites were dangerous things, because they interfered with the dictates of reason. The Stoics also counseled indifference to exterior realities, to pain and pleasure, wealth and poverty. Only virtue mattered.

Though Socrates was not a Stoic himself— he died before Zeno began teaching—the Stoics revered him for the serenity with which he accepted the decision of the Athenian elders to put him to death and the tranquility with which he carried out the sentence on himself. The Roman statesman and Stoic philosopher Seneca would have the chance to imitate Socrates in 65 A.D., when he was accused, perhaps falsely, of taking part in a conspiracy to kill the Emperor Nero, his former pupil. Ordered to commit suicide, he cut his wrists and legs, then slowly bled while calmly issuing last words to his disciples. It was a very stoic ending.

Ancient Greeks Surmise That the World Is Composed of Atoms

12 We think we know when the atomic age began: in the 20th century, with nuclear energy and the atomic bomb. But in a sense it has its origins in the earliest moments of Greek philosophy. Starting in the seventh century B.C., a number of Greek thinkers turned their attention to the same question. "What is the fundamental substance on which all of creation is based?" Thales believed it was water. Anaximenes said air. Heraclitus felt sure it was fire. Eventually, Empedocles would add earth to the mix and diplomatically suggest that the universe rested on all of the above.

But from a modern perspective, the most interesting speculations were made by Leucippus and his follower Democritus, who lived in the fifth century B.C. They believed that everything was made of something they called "atoms"—from the Greek meaning "cannot be divided." Atoms were invisible, indestructible, separated by empty space and in constant motion. Sometimes they collided and bounced off one another like billiard balls. Sometimes they combined and interlocked, which would be a fair way to describe what we now call molecules. In the end they were the invisible building blocks of all things, even the soul, which Democritus said consisted of spherical atoms of fire. And to the extent that science now tells us that the universe is a bristling world of infinitesimal particles, the Greek "atomists" were right.

Socrates Develops a Powerful Means of Pursuing the Truth

13 It's just one of the ironies of the life and legacy of Socrates (c. 470–399 B.C.) that while he's one of the most famous names in the history of philosophy, he never produced a single book. Most of what we know of him we find in the work of his student Plato, who presents us again and again with a picture of Socrates engaging others in probing dialogues, talking with whoever would listen. Concerned with the practical questions of how people should live their lives, his most fundamental contribution to the history of ideas wasn't any particular answer but simply the way he went about examining these issues. It was through a series of questions and replies leading to more questions, asked in such a way as to challenge settled assumptions and illuminate the sources of belief. What is beauty? he would ask. What is the good? What is love? It's a technique we now call the "Socratic method," and it's widely used in teaching to this day.

Encouraging people to question everything is never a good way to ingratiate yourself with the powers that be. In 399 B.C., when he was about 70, Socrates was arrested on charges of corrupting Athenian youth and failing to believe in the Athenian gods. He was convicted and eventually sentenced to death by drinking hemlock. His trial, final philosophical speculations, and his death were all recorded by Plato years later in three works, *Apology, Crito,* and *Phaedo.* It's in the first of these that Socrates offers the simplest explanation for his constant questioning, an explanation that has served ever since as the fundamental justification of philosophy itself: "The unexamined life is not worth living."

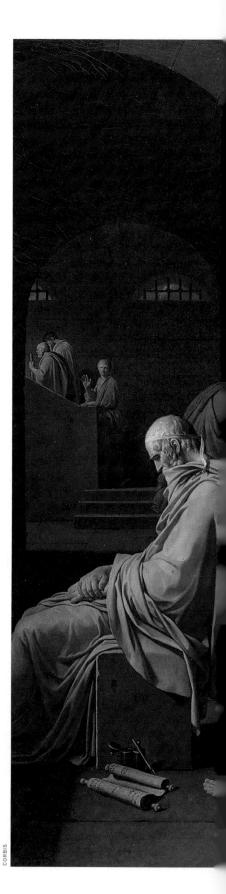

LAST WORDS *In Jacques-Louis David's* The Death of Socrates, *from 1787, the philosopher urges his pupils to focus on higher things as he reaches for the fatal cup of hemlock.*

SCHOOL IS IN SESSION *A first-century floor mosaic uncovered at Pompeii, in Italy, depicts Plato's school in Athens, the Academy.*

Plato Proposes a World of Ideal Forms

14 Imagine the following situation. "Human beings living in an underground cave, which has a mouth open towards the light and reaching all along the cave. Here they have been from their childhood, and have their legs and necks chained so that they cannot move, and can only see before them, being prevented by the chains from turning round their heads."

Wait! It gets even stranger. Above and behind the chained people, a fire is blazing at a distance, and between the fire and the prisoners there is a raised pathway with a low wall. Along the wall men are walking and carrying things like statues and bowls. The fire throws the shadows of those men and things onto the wall that the chained people are facing. Those shadows are the only sights the chained people see and all they know of reality. But of course what they're seeing is not reality, but merely the shadows of real things.

This odd little vignette is the "Allegory of the Cave." It appears in *The Republic,* the most famous book by the philosopher Plato (427–347 B.C.). He uses the story to illustrate his theory that the world we perceive with our senses is not reality but a kind of shadow, a dim copy of larger realities—he calls them Forms or Ideas—that are invisible and eternal. So, for instance, all individual beds are merely imperfect expressions of an eternal Idea of "bed." Qualities—beauty, goodness, even tallness—are also merely expressions of eternal Forms that cannot be apprehended by the senses but can be grasped by reason.

Plato's doctrine of ideal Forms would lay the basis for all subsequent metaphysics (the search for absolute truth in a realm outside the physical world). As British thinker Alfred North Whitehead once said, "The safest characterization of the European philosophical tradition is that it consists of a series of footnotes to Plato."

Aristotle Arrives at a Way to Think

15 The third towering figure of Greek philosophy is Aristotle (384–322 B.C.), a student of Plato. After traveling around the Mediterranean world, he returned to Athens in the last 13 years of his life and established a school called the Lyceum. Aristotle delved into multiple areas of knowledge, including mathematics, biology, politics, physics, and ethics. But his most important contribution may have been his invention of logic. He was the first to develop a system of reasoning, a way of describing how thought might lead to knowledge. His "deductive logic" would dominate Western ways of thinking until the Renaissance.

How does it work? At the heart of Aristotle's system was something he called a "syllogism." That was his word for a form of argument from the general to the particular that consisted of three parts: a major premise, a minor premise, and a conclusion. In any syllogism, as long as the premise is true, then the conclusion —or "deduction"—must also be true.

One of Aristotle's most famous examples of a syllogism goes this way.

1. The major premise: All men are mortal.
2. The minor premise: Socrates is a man.
3. The conclusion—drumroll, please— Therefore, Socrates is mortal.

Aristotle believed that all knowledge begins with the experience of the senses. But his syllogisms always begin with first premises that are assumed to be true and do not need to be proved. Aristotle believed they were "self-evident," meaning they were obviously true once you understood them. This could put his reasoning on somewhat shaky ground. It became a matter of arriving at truth largely through mental processes that did not always need to be tested against the real world.

Aristotle's logic would prove hugely influential for the next 2,000 years. But by the late Middle Ages its enduring authority was an obstacle to the rise of the physical sciences, which begin with observed facts and then proceed to draw probable conclusions from those. As late as 1945, British philosopher Bertrand Russell could still complain: "Throughout modern times, practically every advance in science, in logic, or in philosophy has had to be made in the teeth of the opposition from Aristotle's disciples."

DEBATERS *Plato and Aristotle dispute in a 15th-century carved relief by Luca della Robbia, from the Campanile of the Church of Santa Maria del Fiore in Florence.*

Does the Universe Go On Forever?

16 The Greek mathematician Pythagoras had a very cozy picture of the universe. The earth was at the center, surrounded by a series of ever larger crystalline spheres that held the sun, the moon, the stars, and the other planets. Each body was attached to its own sphere, which moved around the earth, the body moving with it. As the spheres turned, each made a characteristic tone—a musical note. As they all turned together, they produced a perfect harmony—the music of the spheres.

What caused the spheres to move? Aristotle reasoned that, since the earth was stationary, it couldn't be the thing responsible for setting them in motion. It must be that the movement of the largest, outermost sphere caused the next smaller sphere to move as well, and so on down through each concentric sphere. But who moved the largest sphere? Aristotle's answer was something he called the "prime mover," which Christian thinkers would identify as God.

The universe described by Pythagoras and Aristotle was finite. The outermost sphere, where the stars were attached, was the last one. Beyond that there was only the prime mover. Centuries later, Copernicus would demonstrate that the earth was not the center of the universe. Instead, it circled around the sun. With that he did more than redraw the map of the solar system. He opened the floodgates of speculation about infinity. If the earth was not the center of the universe, was it not possible that space went on forever, an endless stream of stars and planets and the vast stretches between them?

Scientists still don't have the answer, though the information they have increasingly persuades them to lean toward an infinite model. The latest data has been gathered by the Wilkinson Microwave Anistropy Probe—WMAP—a spacecraft launched in 2001 by NASA to make fundamental measurements of the universe, including its geometry. The WMAP probe stopped collecting information in the summer of 2010, and analysis of its last two years of findings is expected to be complete in 2012. Will those definitively settle the matter of whether the universe is infinite? Or is it a question more likely to go on forever?

AS THE WORLDS TURN *In 1493, the German historian Hartmann Schedel published his illustrated* World Chronicle. *It included this image of an enclosed universe of heavenly spheres.*

The Epicureans Discover the Pleasure Principle

17 Pleasure. Is it the purpose of life? The Greek philosopher Epicurus (341–270 B.C.) thought so—in a way. "Pleasure," he said, "is the beginning and the end of the blessed life." But what did he mean by pleasure? The man who could say, "The root of all good is the pleasure of the stomach," was obviously no ascetic. But he believed above all in moderation. Though it's from his name that we take our modern word "epicure," meaning a person with refined taste in food and wine, Epicurus was no epicure himself. He claimed to live almost entirely on bread and water, with the occasional morsel of cheese. "The greatest good of all," he said, "is prudence."

So what he really had in mind when he spoke of pleasure had nothing to do with gluttony or lust or even sensuality. It was the absence of pain, a condition that might best be described as contentment and well-being. He believed in serene enjoyments and counseled his followers to avoid turbulent ones, including sex. "Sexual intercourse has never done a man good," he insisted, "and he is lucky if it has not harmed him." He even recommended staying out of public life. It opened you up to too many excitements and troubling expectations. So forget politics, forget the tumults of love—to him, steady friendship was the ideal social relationship.

What better place to advance a philosophy of quiet contentment than from a garden? So, naturally, that was where Epicurus taught. His garden in Athens became the center of a close-knit community of pupils, one that he opened up to admit slaves and women, something almost unheard of in the ancient world. He instructed them all in a materialist view of the world. Like Democritus, he believed that all things consist of atoms in constant motion. Though he believed in the gods, he insisted they played no role in human affairs, and he utterly rejected the teachings of religion, which he thought promoted falsehood, fear, and unhappiness. All the same, he believed in the existence of the soul, but one that disintegrated when the body died. Therefore, he reasoned, no one needed to fear punishment in an afterlife— there was nothing left to punish.

The Skeptics Ask: Is It Possible to Know Anything With Certainty?

18 How do you know that what you "know" is true? How can you be sure you aren't dreaming everything? Or that your mind hasn't been programmed somehow to believe in a "reality" that is in fact simulated? These questions didn't begin with the sci-fi classic *The Matrix*. They bedeviled some of the earliest Greek philosophers and have continued to preoccupy thinkers ever since.

The first of those inquiring Greeks were the philosophers who called themselves skeptics, a school of thought traceable to Pyrrho of Elis, who was active around 300 B.C. Because he left behind no written record, we know of his work through a much later figure, Sextus Empiricus, a Roman philosopher of the second century A.D., who described Pyrrho's system in one of his books. Like many Greek philosophers, Pyrrho was concerned about the unreliability of knowledge gained through the senses, and concluded that because of that unreliability true knowledge of any kind, including moral and ethical conclusions, is impossible. To put it bluntly—and the skeptics did—it's impossible to make any statement that rests on a firmer foundation than the exact opposite statement. And for that reason, it makes no sense even to prefer one course of action to another, because they both must rest on unprovable assumptions.

In effect, the skeptics took the Socratic method, with its constant questioning of settled beliefs, to its logical extreme—that no belief is to be trusted, no position to be held. It's worth noting that skepticism itself is a "belief," which means that a case could be made in support of its very opposite—unquestioning belief, or dogmatism—and a good skeptic would have to say yes, it could. But the questions about the reliability of knowledge that the ancient skeptics posed proved to be very difficult to bat away. In the 17th and 18th centuries they would return to occupy the minds of some of the greatest European philosophers, including René Descartes and David Hume—who would never entirely be able to put them to rest.

CURVACEOUS *At right, a stretch of the aqueducts at Caesarea, on the coast of what is now Israel, part of a system begun in the first century B.C. by King Herod; below, the central aisle of the 12th-century Chapel of San Cataldo in Palermo; above, the interior of the Pantheon in Rome, which was rebuilt around 125 A.D. by the Emperor Hadrian.*

The Romans Perfect a Building Block of Building

19 One way that builders can cover a room or support weight over an entryway is to lay a beam horizontally across two vertical pillars. This kind of "post and beam" construction is among the earliest known building methods, stretching back to Stonehenge and beyond. But it can support only limited weight before the beam sags and cracks under the stress.

The Romans had a better idea—the arch, a curving span made from separate wedge-shaped stones. Those stones joined at the top at a "keystone" that became the focal point of the downward pressure exerted by whatever load the arch was supporting. The Romans didn't invent the arch. They borrowed it from the Greeks, and it had been used by even earlier cultures, including those of Egypt and Mesopotamia. But the Romans found a way to make it bear much larger loads. Essential to that improvement was their invention of a particularly strong variety of concrete, a mixture of rock, lime, and sandy volcanic ash. It made possible arches capable of wide spans, which became a regular feature of the monumental buildings, like the colosseums, that appeared throughout the Roman Empire.

With the arch it also became possible for the Romans to build the long aqueducts that brought water to towns throughout the empire. The grand triumphal arch, erected to mark military victories, became one of the characteristic structures of the imperial age. And it was the arch that eventually made possible the dome, among the chief innovations of Roman architecture and one they brought to perfection in Rome's magnificent Pantheon, still the world's largest unreinforced solid-concrete dome.

Even after the empire declined, the arch lived on. It was a key characteristic of the Romanesque architecture of the early Middle Ages. Later medieval architects adapted it for the pointed arches of Gothic cathedrals. And many of the great arches and domes built by the Romans themselves survive to this day. It was a form meant to last—and it has.

A Powerful Faith Is Founded on Christ

20 There is no doubt that Jesus Christ is one of the most significant individuals in history; perhaps only those other great men of the spirit, Muhammad, Confucius, and Buddha, rival his influence. Today some 2.2 billion Christians believe that Jesus, a Jewish preacher in Roman-occupied Judea, was the Messiah promised in Judaism's Old Testament: the son of God, incarnated as a man whose suffering and death absolve sins and promise eternal life to those who heed his message. His story is told in the four Gospels of Christianity's New Testament, which most scholars regard as true to Christ's message, if not to the exact facts of his life. They tell a story of his divine birth, teachings, miracles, death, and bodily resurrection. And they record his enduring challenge, a radical call to charity, expressed most simply and profoundly in the Sermon on the Mount, and to forgiveness: Christians must love their enemies and forgive those who sin against them.

In its first years, amid grotesque persecution, Christianity was spread across the Roman world through the inspired testimony of the disciples who had known Jesus. By the fourth century, it had become the empire's official religion. When Rome fell, the Catholic Church became the repository not just of Christ's teachings but of civilized values as well, a role it maintained for centuries, weathering a great schism with the Eastern Orthodox Church and a Protestant Reformation that split it into a host of smaller sects. Today, more than 20 centuries after Christ's death, Christianity remains one of the most potent forces in the world.

FIERCE *The Beast With Seven Heads, mentioned in the Book of Revelation, appears in a scene from* The Apocalypse of Angers, *a series of 14th-century tapestries woven by Nicolas Bataille for a castle in Angers, France.*

HE IS RISEN *The belief that the crucified Christ rose from the dead is a central tenet of Christianity. Here it's depicted in Piero della Francesca's famed 15th-century fresco* The Resurrection.

The Great Religions Imagine the End of the World

21 How will the world end? Almost every religion has had something to say on the question. In his Sermon of the Seven Suns, the Buddha says that over a long succession of centuries, six additional suns will appear in the sky until the oceans boil away and the earth ignites into a ball of flame, until "neither ashes nor soot remains." In the Old Testament the prophet Daniel describes a vision in which four beasts emerge from the sea and ravage mankind before being defeated. Then more wonders follow, and great wars that culminate in "a time of trouble" before the final deliverance of Israel. And much of the Koran dwells on a day of judgment "when the mountains vanish (like a mirage)."

But nothing quite compares to the tumultuous final book of the New Testament, the Revelation of John, with its blazing trumpets and seven seals, its locusts with men's faces, and climactic battle of Armageddon. In the end Satan and his lieutenants are cast into a lake of fire, and John sees a new heaven and earth. "Behold," Christ says, "I make all things new." Scholars believe that Revelation was probably written near the end of the first century A.D. by John the Elder, a Christian who had been exiled to the barren Aegean island of Patmos, possibly for practicing his faith. It was a time when the Roman Emperor Domitian required people to worship his family as gods, a demand no Christian could agree to. John may have written his text as a way to encourage Christians to endure whatever persecution they might have to suffer in the faith that Christ—and they—would prevail. But for centuries many Christians have believed that Revelation is a reliable prophecy of just how the world will end. With that in mind, they have examined the events of their own day for signs that, as John warns, "the time is near."

St. Augustine Explains the City of God

22 The fifth century was a time of tremendous upheaval in the Mediterranean world. A fierce Germanic tribe, the Goths, had descended upon Italy. In 410 A.D. they entered and sacked Rome—the beginning of the end of the Western Empire. The fall of Rome left many people angry and perplexed. Thirty years earlier Christianity had been adopted as the official faith of the Empire. Now some complained that the collapse was a punishment for turning away from the old pagan gods.

The most powerful Christian answer to that challenge is *The City of God*, the work of St. Augustine (354–430 A.D.), the Bishop of Hippo, a small Roman city in what is now Algeria. Along with St. Paul, he was the most important early formulator of Church doctrine and one of the first to combine Greek philosophy with Christian theology.

In his book, which he wrote in stages between 412 and 427, Augustine points out first that when the pagan gods were honored they never protected Rome, which had deservedly suffered many wars and famines. Worse still, paganism offers no hope for the protection that matters—eternal salvation. He goes on to define and chart the history of two "cities"—not physical localities but communities of common interest—that co-exist on earth. One is the eternal City of God. Its people are the elect, those preordained by God to spend eternity in heaven because they are the ones he has decided will receive the gift of his grace. The corrupt and decaying Earthly City is made up of all those who will never be saved. Though the two groups will be separated at the Last Judgment, until that day they live in this world mingled together. We cannot know for certain who will be saved. Even they don't know. But we can be sure that there is no hope of salvation for those outside the Church.

With *The City of God*, Augustine offered the first attempt at a comprehensive philosophy of history, one that provided a hugely influential picture of the ways that Christians should think about the purpose of life and their place within society. Above all, he cautions, Christians must live in this world with their eyes constantly on the next and not be seduced by worldly concerns. "God's city lives in this world's city," he writes, "but it lives there as an alien sojourner."

THE PROFESSOR *This painting by Benozzo Gozzoli, one of 16 biographical frescoes in the Church of St. Augustine in San Gimignano, Italy, shows the saint teaching in Rome.*

A WORLD BEHIND WALLS *To preserve its medieval character, the fortified city of Carcassonne, in France, was restored in the 19th century.*

Middle Ages

BEARER OF COMFORT
At left, in a 10th-century illuminated manuscript, Boethius is visited in his prison cell by Lady Philosophy. Below, the title page of a version of Consolation *that was translated into Old English in the ninth century by England's King Alfred the Great.*

AN. MANL. SEVER. BOETHI
Consolationis Philosophiæ
LIBRI V.
ANGLO-SAXONICE REDDITI
AB
ALFREDO,
Inclyto Anglo-Saxonum Rege.

Ad apographum JUNIANUM expreſſos edidit
CHRISTOPHORUS RAWLINSON,
è Collegio Reginæ.

OXONIÆ,
E THEATRO SHELDONIANO MDCXCVIII.
Sumtibus Editoris, Typis JUNIANIS.

A Condemned Man Attempts to Understand God's Ways

23 Boethius (c. 480–524) was a good man who came to a bad end. Born to an aristocratic Roman family, he was fluent in Greek, translated Aristotle into Latin, and wrote treatises on mathematics, philosophy, and music. A member of the Roman Senate in the decades after the barbarians had deposed the last western emperor, he rose to become a high councilor to Theodoric, the Goth king of Italy. But in 524 he was charged, perhaps falsely, with disloyalty and sentenced to death. It was while awaiting execution in a dungeon near Milan that he composed *The Consolation of Philosophy*, which would become one of the most widely read and influential books of the Middle Ages.

Consolation might be described as one of the first "when bad things happen to good people" books. It takes the form of a dialogue between Boethius and Lady Philosophy, who appears to him in his cell. He pours out to her his sense of the injustice of what has happened to him. "If God *is*," he asks, "whence come evil things?" Philosophy replies that he must not expect good fortune to be permanent. And besides, whatever can be snatched away—riches, power, beauty, health—cannot bring ultimate happiness, because the good things in life are mere reflections of the highest good, which is God. Eventually she presents a picture of a universe created by God and filled everywhere with his goodness, but one in which he doesn't step in to set things right in the eyes of ordinary humans. In effect, she tells him that, from the limited perspective of humans, God works in mysterious ways.

Soon after Boethius completed his book, he was executed. Catholic tradition would treat him as a martyr, though he did not die for his faith. But he died *with* his faith—in a God of infinite, if puzzling, goodness.

What Is Free Will? And Do We Have It?

24 It was already a problem in the first book of the Bible. The disobedience of Adam and Eve—eating the forbidden fruit of the Tree of Knowledge—was also the first act of free will, of the power to choose the actions you perform, including the choice to do right or wrong. Given that it got them expelled from paradise, there was plainly only so much free will that God was prepared to tolerate. Yet free will seemed necessary to Christian belief—it would be unjust to punish souls for violating God's law if they had no choice but to do what they did.

Two of the earliest Church fathers, Paul and Augustine, believed that God chose an "elect" whom he knew in advance—because he knew all things—would be saved. But Augustine still believed that people had free will. God did not make them sin—he merely knew in advance which ones would be sinners. The idea of an elect found a more dogmatic restatement in the voice of the stern 17th-century Protestant reformer John Calvin. The Calvinist doctrine of predestination held that the fate of all souls was predetermined, and nothing they might do could alter whether it was their fate to be saved or damned. And by what signs might we know just who the saved were, or if we were among them? Well, they were Calvinists. Some of Calvin's more radical followers maintained that the Fall of Adam and Eve had been foreseen and intended by God, neutralizing even that first act of free will.

Theologians aren't the only ones who have puzzled over free will. Just about every major philosopher has pondered the question. And as the science of genetics advanced, it added a profound twist to the argument: How much of our behavior is predetermined by our genes? If there is a gene that predisposes you to crime, how free are you not to become a criminal? If other genes make you more likely to be loving or left-handed, artistic or alcoholic, how does your free will interact with the chains of DNA that try to bind you? As Eve reached for the apple, how much of what she did was she responsible for?

PICK AND CHOOSE *Adam and Eve prepare to be tempted by Satan, in a 16th-century Vatican fresco by Raphael*

Muhammad's Teachings Shape a New Faith, Islam

25 The Prophet Muhammad was born about 570 A.D. to a member of a respected clan in Mecca, a city in what we now call the Saudi peninsula. By the time he was 6, both his mother and father had died; he was raised by a poor uncle, whose herds he tended. At 25, Muhammad accepted a marriage proposal from Khadijah, a rich Meccan widow 15 years his senior, for whom he had led a successful caravan. With his financial security ensured, he began to venture into the desert to contemplate and pray. There, in a cave at the foot of Mount Hira, a vision came to him: The Angel Gabriel roused him with the stern command, "Proclaim!"

And he did. At 40, Muhammad began preaching the new faith of Islam. Like Judaism and Christianity, it insisted on a single god, Allah. His teachings met with favor from many, but local traders feared his rising influence, as did Christian and Jewish clerics. In 622 he and his followers fled to Medina in a migration known as the Hegira; he soon attracted a growing body of converts. Revelations came to him in trances and were later collected as the Koran. As his disciples grew in numbers, they began a series of raids on Meccan caravans. In 628 the Meccans agreed to let Muhammad's followers make their pilgrimage to the Kaaba, an ancient shrine that Muslims believe was hallowed by the prophet Abraham. Two years later the Prophet led an army of 10,000 into the city, taking control in a bloodless victory. Muhammad died in 632, but Islam's great days were ahead. A political faith with a yearning to expand, it soon expressed a dynamic manifest destiny. Muslims burst out of Arabia to create an empire that stretched across northern Africa and into Spain, and through the Middle East to India and Southeast Asia. Today an estimated 1.5 billion Muslims around the globe pause five times each day to face Mecca and state their credo: "There is but one god, Allah, and Muhammad is his Prophet."

IN THE NAME OF ALLAH *In* The Prayer, *above, a painting from 1865, the French artist Jean-Léon Gérôme shows Muslims engaged in a practice their faith requires them to carry out five times each day. At right, two pages of a 17th-century copy of the Koran.*

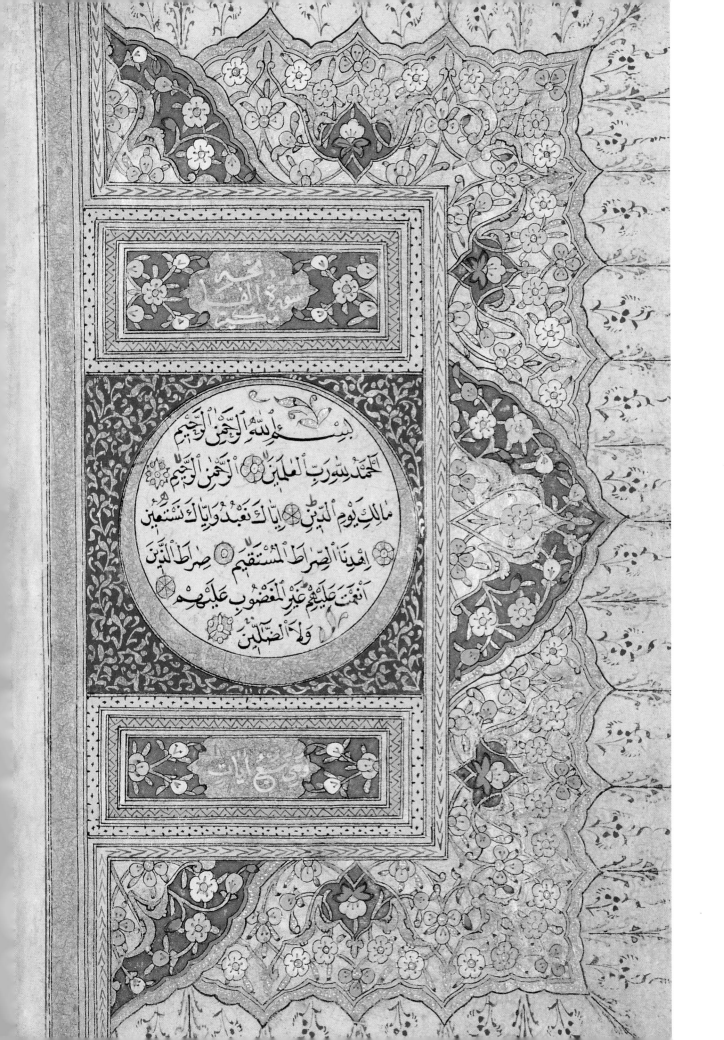

سورة الفاتحة مكية

بِسْمِ اللَّهِ الرَّحْمَٰنِ الرَّحِيمِ
الْحَمْدُ لِلَّهِ رَبِّ الْعَالَمِينَ ۞ الرَّحْمَٰنِ الرَّحِيمِ ۞
مَالِكِ يَوْمِ الدِّينِ ۞ إِيَّاكَ نَعْبُدُ وَإِيَّاكَ نَسْتَعِينُ
۞ اهْدِنَا الصِّرَاطَ الْمُسْتَقِيمَ ۞ صِرَاطَ الَّذِينَ
أَنْعَمْتَ عَلَيْهِمْ غَيْرِ الْمَغْضُوبِ عَلَيْهِمْ
۞ وَلَا الضَّالِّينَ

وهي سبع آيات

Can Images Undermine Truth? Some Would Say So

26 In March 2001, the Taliban regime that ruled Afghanistan stunned the world by destroying two ancient and monumental sculptures of the Buddha carved into the sandstone cliffs of the province of Bamiyan. Images have power—to enchant, but also to threaten. For centuries they have threatened those who believe that images stand in the way of the authentic search for God, and who have retaliated by obliterating religious art. We call that self-inflicted wound iconoclasm, from the Greek *eikono klasmos*—"image breaking."

It has a long history. Jews were discouraged from religious imagery by the injunction against "graven images" in the biblical book of Exodus. Most Moslems have long been opposed to religious imagery, including representations of the Prophet. But hostility to "idol worship" has been a struggle for centuries within Christianity as well. In the year 726 the episode that first gave iconoclasm its name began when Byzantine Emperor Leo III ordered the destruction of all pictures and statuary in Christian churches within his empire. It was an order that set off riots in many places and ignited more than a century of turmoil in the Byzantine Empire before the defenders of holy images gained the upper hand decisively in 842.

As the Protestant Reformation got underway in the 16th century, some reformers opposed what they saw as the worship of pictures and statues among the Catholic faithful. John Calvin's hatred of "heathen" imagery and statuary would lead to a wave of church "cleansings" in the Netherlands in 1566 and campaigns against holy pictures and statues during the English Civil War. It was an attitude the Pilgrims, Puritan followers of Calvin, would carry with them to the New World.

Mathematicians Discover the Power of Zero

27 Zero—to put it mildly, it doesn't seem like much. Yet when it was finally recognized, it revolutionized mathematics. It was first introduced among the Babylonians. Like us, they used a "place holder" system of number notation. When we see a two-digit number like 42, we know that the number in the first column represents tens and in the second column represents ones—so 42 means four tens and two ones. Then write 421 and the same numeral four now appears in the hundreds column, while the two has moved to the tens column to represent two tens: 20.

By contrast, Roman numerals simply string together symbols for various quantities until they arrive at the representation for the complete number. So 321 is written as CCCXXI. For obvious reasons, multiplication and division using the Roman system was quite a challenge. All the same, the Babylonians had a problem too. They lacked a zero—a numeral to represent the absence of quantity the way a zero in 401 means there are no tens in that number. Instead they left an empty space between numerals, which could lead to confusion. But sometime after 2000 B.C., they adopted a mark to represent absence. Though it wasn't the oval we use today, zero was born, at least as a concept, and with it a much more efficient means of making calculations.

It took this idea centuries to be accepted by the West, but by the ninth century, zero had also emerged in India. It flowed back West because by that time the Arabs had invaded India, adopted the Indian numeral system—what we now call Arabic numerals—and introduced it to Europe. And with that, zero, and all its many possibilities, had finally arrived.

THE BRIDGEMAN ART LIBRARY/GETTY IMAGES

GOING AFTER THE GRAVEN IMAGES
A 17th-century Flemish oil painting on wood panel shows a work of devotional art on the brink of being destroyed by armed men.

China Discovers How to Have a Blast

28 *Huo yao,* the Chinese called it—the fire drug. The discovery of gunpowder grew out of Chinese interest in alchemy, which in China was focused on finding an elixir of eternal life. In experiments with saltpeter, alchemists stumbled upon its explosive qualities when mixed with sulfur and dried honey, which was a source of carbon. A waste product of bacteria that feed on decaying organic matter, saltpeter was widely available in southern China, where it appeared as a crust of white nitrate that could be extracted from topsoil. Eventually charcoal was introduced as a more efficient source of carbon. Light the lethal mixture and a blast follows. "The resulting explosion will stun every soul," as one commentator described it, "and shatter everything around it."

The Chinese perfected gunpowder around the 10th and 11th centuries. At first it was used merely for pyrotechnic displays—a mild explosion, a burst of flame, and a cloud of white smoke. But in time the Chinese learned deadlier uses. Wrap the powder in paper around an arrow, attach a fuse and light it—now it's a "fire arrow." Already aware that packing the powder into a small paper container produced a firecracker, in the 12th century they learned to pack it into larger, hardened containers to produce bombs that they would give names like "Bandit-Burning, Vision-Confusing Magic Fire-Ball."

Late in the 13th century, the Chinese mastered the art of packing gunpowder in a metal tube with an open end to launch bits of metal and crockery at high speed—the first guns. Make guns heavier and mount them on wheels, and you have the first cannons, as the Chinese soon did. And in the century that followed, gunpowder migrated to Europe, where it transformed medieval warfare, giving armies the power to blast through the walls of besieged castles.

Courts Demand That Detentions Conform to the Rule of Law

29 The "Great Writ" of habeas corpus—it's a simple idea with enormous power. Since the Middle Ages, courts have claimed the authority to order that anyone being held in custody must be brought before them, and that the person or authority holding the detainee must show cause why the prisoner's liberty is being denied. If no sufficient reason is offered, the person being held must be set free. Habeas corpus (Latin for "have (or produce) the body") is a basic guarantee of liberty

BOMBS BURSTING IN AIR *In this 13th-century Japanese painting, a mounted samurai charges Mongol invaders from China as shells explode overhead.*

and a fundamental element of all legal systems that have sources in English common law. The writ first emerged there in the early Middle Ages. No exact year is known, though we know it precedes the Magna Carta in 1215 because it is referred to indirectly in the portion that reads "no free man shall be taken or imprisoned…or exiled or in any way ruined…except by the judgment of his peers or by the law of the land." European civil law has no comparable provision, and some legal historians argue that the Magna Carta was itself a response to the inroads made by European civil law into English common law following the Norman conquest of England in 1066. In

1679 the English Parliament formally adopted the writ in the Habeas Corpus Act. In the next century it would be the subject of a prominent clause in the U.S. Constitution, the sole individual right included in the main body of the document, before the Bill of Rights was appended.

Over the years, habeas corpus has been held to apply to many kinds of imprisonment by government authority, including incarceration, post-arrest detention in a local police station, involuntary commitment to a mental hospital, and quarantine—and even situations in which the detainee is being held by another private citizen. It is, very simply, the freedom to be set free.

Verdicts Should Be Decided by a Panel of One's Fellow Citizens

30 One institution of government that most people will take part in at some time is the jury trial. It's a system with sources in medieval England, especially in actions by King Henry II, who ruled from 1154 to 1189. To settle disputes over land and inheritance, Henry introduced the practice of "assizes." Twelve local men with knowledge of the dispute would be called to testify as to who was the rightful owner or heir. They differed from a modern jury in that they were expected to arrive in court already knowing the facts of the case, instead of having evidence for the two sides presented to them there.

In Henry's time, people suspected of crimes were subjected to trial by ordeal. In one variety, a priest would be summoned to bless a pond or river, and the accused would be thrown in. If he or she floated, guilt would be assumed, since the blessed water had "rejected" them. In 1215 the church forbade clergymen to assist in trial by ordeal. That decision delegitimized the procedure, which rested on an assumption that God protected the innocent. So the assize panels were adapted to serve as something more like modern juries—bodies that decide guilt and innocence, and by the 15th century they were more commonly hearing evidence presented to them in court rather than working entirely on the basis of their own information about the case. Though the right to a jury trial is guaranteed in the U.S. Constitution, juries have become less common in the land of their birth. In England, both civil and criminal cases are now more likely to be tried before judges alone.

The Magna Carta Imposes Limits on the Power of Kings

31 By the year 1214, King John of England had given his people any number of reasons to be unhappy. There was his loss of English territory in wars with France and the heavy taxes he imposed to pay for them. There was also the dispute with Pope Innocent III that led to a papal interdict temporarily barring the English from full participation in the rites of the Church. So that year a number of his most powerful barons entered into a rebellion against him. By December the rebels had entered the city of London. On June 15, 1215, the king rode out to meet them on a field outside London called Runnymede. There they forced him to sign the agreement that would come to be known as Magna Carta, or Great Charter. It included guarantees of rule by law and even of a council of 25 barons who could overrule the king if he violated provisions of the Charter.

Very soon after signing the Great Charter, John disavowed it, plunging England into the civil strife called the Barons' War, in which his exasperated nobles sought to dethrone him entirely. That proved unnecessary. He died in 1216, and in time, his son Henry III would allow a revised form of the Charter (significantly, without mention of the council of barons) to be issued under his name. With that, the Charter and the rights it guaranteed began to enter the bloodstream of English law and from there become fundamental to the modern notion of free societies.

SIGNED, SEALED, DELIVERED *In an illustration from a 1911 history of England, King John signs the Magna Carta as his rebellious barons look on.*

BENE SCPSISTI DME THOMMA

SANCTVS THOMAS DE ICA...

ARISTO
TILES

PLATO

VERITAE
MEDITA
TVR GVT
VR MEVM ET
LABRA MEA
DE ESTAEBVN
TVR IMPV
PROVERBIO

MVLTITVD
INIS VSVS
QVE IN P E
BVS NOMI
NANDIS S
EQVENDV P
HILOSOPHV P
CESET EMVNT

VERE HIC
EST LVME
ECCLESIE

HIC ADINVENI
OMNEM VIA DISCIPLINE

Thomas Aquinas Seeks to Reconcile Reason and Faith

32 | After the fall of Rome, many works of Greek philosophy, mathematics, and medicine were lost to thinkers in Europe for centuries. They were preserved, however, in the great centers of learning of the Arab world, which produced a host of Arabic translations and learned commentaries. By the 12th century, those books were becoming available again in the West, especially the work of Aristotle. Such was the persuasive power of his thinking that harmonizing faith and reason became an urgent task within the Church, one that occupied many of the best minds of the century between 1150 and 1250.

The greatest of those was the Dominican priest St. Thomas Aquinas (c. 1225–74). The son of an Italian count, he was educated at universities in Naples, Cologne, and Paris before returning in 1259 to Italy, where in time he embarked on one of his most important works, the *Summa Theologica*. It was in that book that he offered his famous five proofs of God's existence. The first is premised on the idea that all change is caused by something, which in its turn is also caused by something. But because the line of connection cannot go back endlessly, there must be something at the beginning that causes change but does not suffer it. That something, he concludes, is God. The second proof rests on similar grounds: All things are caused, but there must be a First Cause, which is God. The third proof holds that something must always have existed, because had there been nothing, it would have been impossible for anything to emerge from it. What has always existed is God. The fourth proof states that all qualities (hotness, softness) are a reflection of some perfect version of that quality. Goodness must be a reflection of the perfect good, which is God. Finally, all things have some purpose, which implies that some intelligence is guiding them to it. Who might that be? God.

Though modern philosophers have poked many holes in the systems of Aquinas, in 1879 they were formally embraced by Pope Leo XIII, and they remain the most systematic attempt to bridge the gap between philosophy and religion.

THE THINKER *In Benozzo Gozzoli's* The Triumph of St. Thomas Aquinas, *from 1471, Aquinas is flanked by Aristotle and Plato, while the Evangelists work away above him.*

Mysticism Pursues a Direct Route to God

33 "The pain was so sharp that it made me utter several moans; and so excessive was the sweetness caused me by this intense pain that one can never wish to lose it, nor will one's soul be content with anything less than God." That was the Spanish-born St. Teresa of Avila (1515–82), describing one of the most famous experiences in the literature of mysticism: the moment when an angel piereced her heart with an arrow, filling her soul with God's love. Most religious experience takes place in the realm of ordinary consciousness, a realm that comprehends things like doctrine, scripture, and ritual. But from earliest times many religions have developed a strain of mysticism, the attempt to find direct communion with God or some other ultimate reality.

The ancient Greek religion had its Orphic mysteries and ecstatic bacchantes, the frenzied worshippers of the god of wine, Dionysus (or Bacchus, as he was known in Roman religion). Mystical ideas pervade Hinduism. Within the Buddhist tradition there is Zen , with its goal of *satori,* the instantaneous and intuitive grasp of a reality "beyond forms." By the 10th century, Sufism had emerged as a mystical dimension of Islam, best known to Westerners through the work of the great Persian poet Omar Khayyàm and the whirling worship ceremonies of the Dervishes. Thirteenth-century Spain produced the *Kabbalah*, a form of Jewish mysticism based on an esoteric reading of sacred tests.

Christian mysticism flourished in Europe in the late Middle Ages—the very centuries of the great attempt to prove the articles of Christian faith through reason and the logic of Aristotle. Typical was the moment of mystical transport in which St. Francis of Assisi (c. 1181–1226) received the stigmata, wounds corresponding to the ones suffered by Christ on the cross. In 1418 the German monk Thomas à Kempis (c. 1380–1471) produced *The Imitation of Christ*, a classic work of devotional exercises aimed at arriving at a union with God. Like Teresa, some mystics experience God with an almost erotic charge. It was to describe the tongues of fire that she said had descended on her from heaven that the German nun Hildegard of Bingen (1098–1179), a poet, used these rapturous words: "O fire of love. O sweet draught in the breast and flooding of the heart ..."

TOUCHED BY GOD In St. Francis of Assisi in Ecstasy, *a painting from around 1595 , the Italian master Caravaggio shows Francis assisted by an angel at the moment he receives the stigmata.*

A REBIRTH OF THE ARTS The Journey of the
Magi to Bethlehem, *part of a fresco from around
1460 by the Florentine painter Benozzo Gozzoli*

Renaissance

LA PRIMAVERA *Sandro Botticelli's painting from around 1482 bears many signs of the Renaissance rediscovery of the Classical world.*

Humanism Makes Man "The Measure of All Things"

34 The Middle Ages had a very gloomy view of life on earth, which the Church saw merely as something to be gotten through as preparation for the eternal life after death. But by the mid-14th century, thinkers with a new view of things were accumulating in parts of Europe, especially in Italy. "Humanism," as this new attitude would eventually be called, would become the defining intellectual characteristic of the emerging European Renaissance.

It began with books, with the rediscovery by thinkers, writers, and men of independent means of the classical texts of antiquity, especially Latin works like Virgil's epic poem *The Aeneid* and the writings and speeches of the Roman statesman Cicero. (The Italian poet Petrarch, one of the earliest and most ardent humanists, once wrote that he could not read Cicero "without kissing the book.") Inspired by what they read, the humanists gradually took on the outlook of the ancient Greeks and Romans they so admired. They came to reject the Church's view of men and women primarily as sinful creatures in need of salvation through God's grace. Instead they emphasized the dignity of the human race, the greatest achievement of the God-created universe. ("Imagine!" wrote Giovanni Pico della Mirandola, the consummate Italian humanist. "The great generosity of God! The happiness of man! To man it is allowed to be whatever he chooses to be!") The humanists valued worldly pleasures. They were devoted to beauty (including the beauty of nature, which they were among the first Europeans to notice), to the arts, and to eloquent speech. They rejoiced at individuality, which the medieval Church discouraged. And they promoted the idea of free scientific inquiry, uninhibited by Church dogma, helping to create an intellectual climate that was open to new discoveries.

Later Generations Rediscover the Civilizations of Ancient Greece and Rome

35 Down through the centuries, the classical ideal has haunted the Western imagination. Again and again, artists and architects have returned to the works of ancient Greece and Rome to find inspiration and validation. The term for that recurring quest is classicism (or sometimes neoclassicism). Its first great moment was the Italian Renaissance, when pagan gods and goddesses were recruited everywhere into literature and art. In architecture, Brunelleschi, Bramante, and Michelangelo adopted elements of Roman construction—the arch, the dome, the column and pediment—for great projects like Il Duomo in Florence and St. Peter's Basilica in Rome. Classical ideals of the human form were revered. Michelangelo's *David* would be unthinkable without the example of ancient statuary. There would be another neoclassical moment in the 17th century, much of it because of the French painter Nicolas Poussin, who relocated to Rome to study firsthand the monuments of antiquity, and by way of his work conveyed back into French art a poise and clarity that would characterize it for almost a century.

Classicism can serve many purposes. It can be a palate cleanser, a way to restore simplicity and clarity after a period of artistic excess. Thus, in the 18th century, after the congested ornament of the Rococo period, English architecture took a sharp turn toward classical models. Classicism can also be used to give ancient authority to new social and political arrangements. To associate the French Revolution with the manly virtues of antiquity, the French painter Jacques-Louis David produced scenes from ancient history in a spare, spot-lit manner. And across the Atlantic, neoclassical style for government buildings announced the ancient roots of the newborn American democracy.

CLASSIC *With its columned porch and its dome inspired by the Pantheon, the Villa Capra in Vicenza, Italy, designed by Andrea Palladio and begun in 1566, is a prime example of neoclassical borrowings.*

Western Artists Gain Some Perspective

36 | There's the world, and then there are pictures of the world. Just how to get them to match up confounded people for centuries. Look at the art of the Egyptians. Their wall paintings only show figures in flat profile. Based on the evidence of their painted vases and carved reliefs, however, the Greeks achieved some understanding of how to represent depth and volume. And though we have few surviving examples of painting from the Roman Empire, those that remain demonstrate that the Romans, too, had a serviceable if imperfect means of representing the way things farther from the eye appear smaller than those closer.

But like so many of the discoveries of the ancient world, with the fall of the empire, the Western world lost the crucial drawing technique we call perspective. This is the ability to represent three-dimensional objects and space on a two-dimensional surface so that they appear with respect to their size, position, and distance from the eye, just as they would if viewed in real space from a particular point.

TO THE POINT *At left, an image from an artist's treatise of 1604 illustrates the principles of single-point perspective; above, a painting from 1667 by Wilhelm van Ehrenberg employs perspective to produce a profound illusion of deep space on the flat surface of a canvas.*

It was not until the mid 14th century that Italian artists began to regain it. Giotto plainly understood how to create believable interiors by slanting overhead features like ceiling rafters downward and floors upward to give the impression that both planes were receding in space. He also used chiaroscuro, the technique of light and shade, to give his figures a sense of three dimensions.

So at the start of the 15th century, the stage was set for the crowning contribution of Filippo Brunelleschi (1377–1436), the Florentine architect who designed the dome of his city's great cathedral. He had also spent time surveying the ruins of ancient Rome, and methods he used in surveying may have helped him to think about how things are best represented in space. It was Brunelleschi who turned perspective into a scientific system, based on the idea of lines converging upon a "vanishing point." From this, the art of the Renaissance burst forward—and backward, into deep, recessional space—opening the way to the beckoning, inward-drawing, and explosive achievements of European painting for centuries to come, as well as those of artists elsewhere who adopted the European discovery. Until the invention of photography, perspective was the most powerful tool mankind possessed for taking visual possession of the world.

Gutenberg Invents the Printing Press

37 When a young German, Johannes Gutenberg (1398–1468), took up his trade, printing was a laborious business. Each new page required the creation of a new printing form, usually an incised block of wood. So he began looking for ways to make metal casts of the individual letters of the alphabet: Equipped with a sufficient supply of them, a printer could use and reuse them in any order required to run off thousands of copies of each page. He solved the technical obstacles, discovering an alloy that would melt at low temperatures (so that it could be poured into letter molds) and an ink that could crisply transfer impressions from metal to paper. He rejiggered a wine press to create the force to print the impressions. Eureka! In 1455, visitors to the Frankfurt Trade Fair reported having seen sections of a Latin Bible with two columns of 42 lines each printed—printed!—on each page. The completed book appeared in 1456 and eventually became known as the Gutenberg Bible.

Before print, the ability to read was restricted to society's elites and the trained scribes who handled their affairs. Affordable books made literacy a crucial skill and an unprecedented means of social advancement for those who acquired it. Established hierarchies began to crumble. Books were the world's first mass-produced items, and printing spurred the greatest extension of human consciousness ever created. It isn't over: The 555-year-old information revolution continues on the Internet, where—thanks to a German printer who wanted a more efficient way to do business—you can read all about it on your iPad.

BAD EXAMPLE *Cesare Borgia, ruler of Urbino, seen here in a 16th-century portrait, served Machiavelli as one model for the kind of unscrupulous tyrant he would write of approvingly in* The Prince.

Machiavelli Develops the Doctrine of Ruthless Power

38 "Whoever becomes the master of a city accustomed to freedom, and does not destroy it, may expect to be destroyed himself." "It is far better to be feared than loved if you cannot be both."

Thus two advisories from *The Prince* by Niccolò Machiavelli (1469–1527), the how-to manual of cold-blooded statecraft. At the age of 29, Machiavelli became "second chancellor" of the Florentine Republic, which required him to travel frequently throughout Italy on diplomatic missions. In those years the Italian peninsula was a patchwork of kingdoms, dukedoms, papal states, and republics, many of them headed by lethal clans—the Medicis, the Sforzas, the Borgias—at constant war with one another. Machiavelli closely observed their world of brutality and double dealing. In 1512, when the Medicis returned to power in Florence, he was imprisoned and tortured. On his release he retreated to his farm outside Florence, where he would write *The Prince.* Not published until 1532, it was a book in the tradition of earlier advisories to rulers. But those typically urged authority to be just, merciful, and trustworthy. Machiavelli sighed and said none of that would do for dealing with the real world, where power is all. The skillful leader must lie when it suits his purposes, spread terror when he needs to, and crush his opponents whenever possible.

Machiavelli effectively separated political theory from ethics—which would turn out to be a captivating idea. Napoleon carried a copy of *The Prince* to the Battle of Waterloo. Hitler claimed to keep one by his bedside. The mobster John Gotti quoted frequently from its pages. But how could any of them resist a book that told them even cruelty was acceptable—so long as it was "well employed"?

IN THE BEGINNING *A page of Gutenberg's Bible. Because color printing would not be invented for centuries, the decorative border was hand-painted.*

Humans Aspire to an Ideal World

39 Utopia. The word was coined by Sir Thomas More (1478–1535) and was the title for his famous tale, published in 1516, about an ideal society on a fictional island. But the utopian impulse— the desire to imagine and, better still, to create, a perfect social order is much older, an age-old human dream of earthly paradise.

The irony, of course, is that most of these ideal worlds would be terrible places to live. The earliest of them was proposed by Plato in *The Republic*, which he completed sometime in the late fourth century B.C. Plato decides that in his just state, the population will be divided into three groups: the common people, the military, and a small elite he calls "the guardians." There's complete equality of the sexes and almost no private property—the guardians live communally—but also not much freedom. The guardians are the only citizens who have political power, and they exert rigid censorship of books and music. Playwrights are banished, and mothers are even expected to tell their children only the bedtime stories authorized by the state.

The ideal community in More's *Utopia* (a word taken from the Greek for "no place") has some similarities with Plato's. Men and women live as equals, and all property is held in common. But the prince who rules the place is elected and can be dismissed. It's also a world of utter conformity—all cities are built to the same plan, and all houses look the same. Everyone wears the same clothes, like the Chinese under Chairman Mao.

Not all utopias have been in books. In the U.S. in the 19th century, there was a boom in religious and secular utopian communities like Brook Farm in Massachusetts, which foundered after six years, and the Oneida community, which survived for more than three decades in upstate New York. In truth, utopian impulses have never managed to produce a real-world paradise for long, if at all. With its promise of a classless society and the withering away of the state, communism had a strong utopian element, but it never succeeded in producing a corresponding reality.

A PERFECT LITTLE WORLD *A tinted woodcut from a 1518 edition of* Utopia *provides an overhead view of the island where Thomas More set his tale of an ideal community.*

LEADERS OF THE OPPOSING SIDES *Martin Luther, above, in a portrait from 1539 by Lucas Cranach the Elder; below, a woodcut by Cranach from an anti-Vatican pamphlet, showing a corrupt Pope selling indulgences, a practice condemned by the Protestant reformers.*

Luther Leads a Revolt Against Rome

40 "Arise, O Lord, and judge thy cause. A wild boar has invaded thy vineyard."

So began the bull, or papal letter, in which Pope Leo X demanded that Augustinian friar Martin Luther (1483–1546) recant his preachings against the Roman Catholic Church's selling of indulgences as a means of buying divine favor. Luther had bravely nailed his 95 Theses arguing against such practices on the door of the Wittenberg Castle church in Saxony on Oct. 31, 1517. But the Vatican couldn't make the wild boar budge. "Here I stand," Luther is said to have declared at the Diet of Worms, the council called by Emperor Charles V to judge him. "I cannot do otherwise. God help me."

Luther's stand against a Church that had become corrupt, arrogant, and rigidly hierarchical was the first salvo in the Protestant Reformation. Inspired by his stand, reformers across Europe now found the courage to question the authority of the Vatican. And that meant questioning the entire apparatus of medieval society, which was founded upon unswerving devotion to the Church and its leaders. As Luther's revolt progressed, he joined others in arguing for the use of vernacular tongues rather than Latin, and he worked to bring education to peasants formerly excluded from schools by religious authorities.

The German rebel rejected centuries of religious dogma to argue that each person—not the Church—was responsible for his or her own salvation. This insistence on the primacy of what he called "personal thinking" over received authority was the Reformation's great contribution to the modern world, paving the way for a new individualism in Western culture. As for the "wild boar," he was excommunicated, and the former friar's revolt against Church teaching was so thorough that he eventually married a former nun. Luther was no saint, but by taking a stand and sticking to it, he moved the world.

Copernicus Turns the Cosmos Around

41 For many centuries, the idea that the sun revolved around the earth, as described in the cosmology of the Greek astronomer Ptolemy, was literally an article of faith—a teaching of the Catholic Church, which saw in it corroboration that the earth was God's creation and the center of his universe. Ironically, it was a Polish churchman, Nicolaus Copernicus (1473–1543), a man of mostly orthodox beliefs, who exploded that settled notion. As a young man he studied in Krakow, Poland, but also at the universities in Bologna and Padua, where he would have been able to absorb the revived learning and new spirit of the Italian Renaissance.

On returning to Poland in 1503, Copernicus became a canon in the cathedral city of Frauenburg and an avid part-time astronomer. Based on his reading of ancient manuscripts and his close observation of the skies—often from the tower of his church—he came early to believe that the earth revolves around the sun and also that it rotates once every 24 hours. But though he allowed his views to be circulated by various means, Copernicus held off on publishing them out of concern for offending the Church. He finally published his most important work, *On the Revolution of the Celestial Spheres,* in 1543—conveniently, the year of his death, which put him out of harm's way. The book was also diplomatically dedicated to Pope Paul III and included a preface by his friend Osiander, assuring readers that the ideas it contained were put forth strictly as a hypothesis.

Copernicus escaped censure by the Church. The Italian astronomer and mathematician Galileo (1564–1642), working in the next century, was not so lucky. Using the newly invented telescope, by 1615 he had confirmed the Copernican theories to his own satisfaction. One year later Copernicus's book was put on the Church's Index of Forbidden Works. Galileo was warned to disavow the Copernican system, which he did—until 1632, when he took it up again. That led him to be called before the Inquisition, the special Church court formed to interrogate heretics, which forced him to recant and sentenced him to house arrest, where he remained for the rest of his life. Not until 1992 would a papal commission conclude that Galileo's judges were guilty of "subjective error."

AS THE WORLD TURNS *An image from a 17th-century "Celestial Atlas" depicts the solar system described by Copernicus, with the sun at its center and the earth revolving around it.*

AN AGE OF SCIENTIFIC INQUIRY
An Experiment on a Bird in the Air Pump, *from 1768, by the British painter Joseph Wright of Derby*

Science Obtains Its Own Method for Arriving at Knowledge

42 Francis Bacon (1561–1626) was a man of the world—the legal world, the political world, the world of letters. A member of Parliament at the age of 23, he would even for a time become Lord Chancellor of England, the office that oversaw the nation's courts, until he was accused of the very worldly crime of accepting bribes. So perhaps it's fitting that he should be credited with arriving at a means of inquiring into truth that depends upon observing the actual world and coming to conclusions based on those observations. We call it inductive reasoning, and it was a crucial early step toward establishing the scientific method.

Bacon believed in God but also believed that philosophy must be entirely divorced from religion and based only upon reason. And he proposed that thinking must begin by observing physical realities, collecting data based on those observations, and drawing narrow conclusions from that data. It's what we now call the empirical method, and it's essential to much modern science. It could be said, however, that Bacon's model doesn't give enough room to the way scientists often begin, not with data but with a hypothesis—an idea they believe might be true—then they gather data and perform experiments to test the hypothesis.

Bacon is also perhaps the first thinker to have conceived the idea of what we would now call technological progress, of an improved future that would be the result of the steady advance of scientific knowledge and of the useful inventions that the sciences would make possible. "Knowledge is power" is a phrase that is said to have originated with him, and he believed that applied knowledge would lead to a better world. He was certainly devoted to the experimental methods he championed, so much so that he died of pneumonia that he is believed to have contracted when he was conducting an experiment in the use of cold as a preservative—by stuffing a chicken with snow.

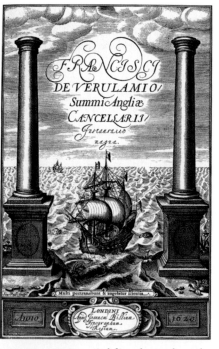

METHOD MAN *Bacon (at left) made crucial contributions to the emergence of scientific thinking. Above, the title page of his most important, though never completed, work,* Instauratio Magna, *from 1620, in which he developed his model of inductive reasoning.*

THE SUN KING *Pierre Mignard's* Equestrian Portrait of Louis XIV Crowned by Victory *captures the spirit of royal absolutism.*

Kings Get Welcome News—Their Powers Derive From God

43 *L'état, c'est moi.* "I am the state." Legend has it that was the famous boast of the Sun King, Louis XIV of France (1638–1715). Whether or not he ever spoke those exact words, they sum up what Louis was pleased to believe. He ruled during the supreme moment of royal absolutism, when kingly prerogatives had expanded to new dimensions, and not just in France. One succinct rationale for that power was put forward by Jacques-Bénigne Bossuet (1627–1704), a French bishop and theologian, who formulated the idea we call the Divine Right of Kings. He developed it in his treatise "On the Nature and Properties of Royal Authority," composed in 1679 as part of a longer text designed for the instruction of Louis's son, the Dauphin, whom Bossuet served as tutor. Bossuet argued that monarchs were the representatives of God on earth and must be obeyed so that God's will might be done. By the same token, kings could not be answerable to any merely human authority. They answered only to God.

France was not the only nation in which the monarch was offered this agreeable proposition. In England in 1680, during the reign of Charles I, Sir Robert Filmer (1588–1653) published *Patriarcha: or The Natural Power of Kings,* in which he argued that God had bestowed royal power upon Adam, and that it descended from him to later kings. Though Charles was no doubt delighted, he might have done better to be a bit skeptical about the broad claims being made for royal authority. Charles exercised it so flagrantly that in 1649, after his defeat in the climax of the English Civil War, he was convicted of high treason and beheaded.

Descartes Hits on a Way to Prove His Own Existence

44 The single most famous proposition in the history of philosophy is one put forward by the French mathematician and philosopher René Descartes (1596–1650): *Cogito ergo sum*. It's Latin for "I think, therefore I am." It represents a radical solution to the problem of radical doubt first put forward by the ancient Greek Skeptics—how can we be certain that anything we know is true?

In *Meditations on First Philosophy*, published in 1642 and considered the starting point of modern philosophy, Descartes set himself the task of putting his own knowledge on a firm foundation. To do that, he decided, he must doubt everything that it is possible to doubt and to accept as true only those things of which he can be absolutely certain. He starts with the evidence of the senses. Those can deceive, no? The sun, for instance, is in fact much larger than it appears to be. And while he may believe that he is sitting near the fire, how can he be sure he's not dreaming it? So "knowledge" based upon the senses must be discounted. Then he considers things that he thinks he knows through his thought processes—for instance, that 2 plus 3 equals 5. But how does he know that a demon isn't making him mistake false thoughts for self-evident truths?

It's at this point that Descartes arrives at his only certainty—he knows that he exists, because *someone* must be thinking his doubting thoughts. "While I wanted to think everything false," he concludes, "it must necessarily be that I who thought was something." At last he has found his rock. "This truth, 'I think, therefore I am,' was so solid and so certain that all the most extravagant suppositions of the Skeptics were incapable of upsetting it." To this day, "Cartesian Doubt" shapes the discussion of knowledge and what we really know about it.

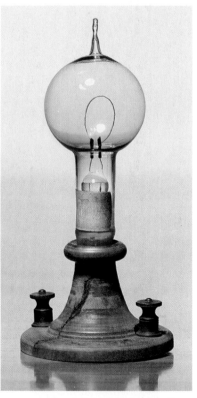

LET THERE BE LIGHTBULBS *A carbon-filament lamp from 1879 of the type perfected by the multitalented American Thomas Edison*

Electricity Crackles to Life

45 One of the fundamental forces that makes modern life possible, electricity was not "discovered" all at once. Rather, it emerged through a series of discoveries that coaxed it into the world and tamed it. As early as the sixth century B.C., the Greek philosopher Thales knew how to generate an electrical charge by rubbing a piece of amber—what the Greeks called *elektron*. But it wasn't until around 1660 that the German physicist Otto von Guericke developed an electrostatic generator—a device that produced static electricity through friction created by rubbing a rotating sulfur ball.

Von Guericke had little idea of to what use electricity might be put. By the mid-18th century, it was still mostly the stuff of stage tricks performed by traveling "electricians" who might do things like send a charge through a line of men holding hands to make them jump. Enter the American patriot and scientist Benjamin Franklin (1706–90). In the late 1740s he learned how to use an electrostatic generator not so different from the one von Guericke had toyed with to collect a charge that he could study. Very soon he had concluded that electricity consisted of two charges, positive and negative. Generating a positive charge would produce an equal negative charge. He also found a way to store electricity by wiring together a series of glass plates with metal on each side that he charged. He gave the device a name: an "electrical battery."

In 1800 the Italian scientist Alessandro Volta made a significant advance with his "voltaic pile," the first true battery, a stack of zinc and copper disks separated by cardboard soaked in brine that produced its own electric charge. The stage was now set for the breakthroughs that would culminate in the lightbulb perfected by Thomas Edison in 1879, and for the world to feel the power of this long-mysterious force.

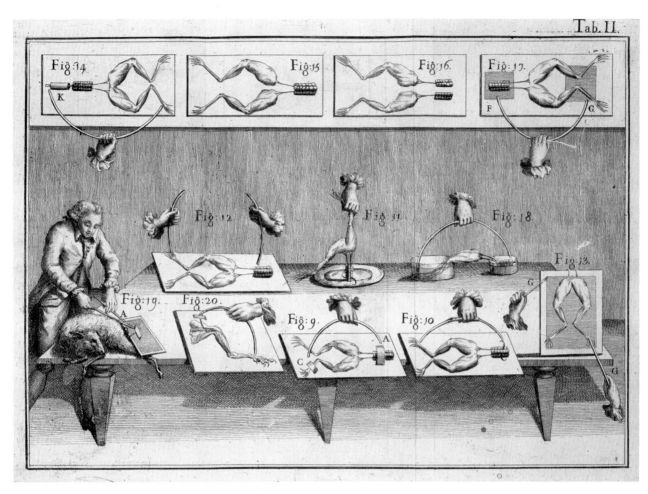

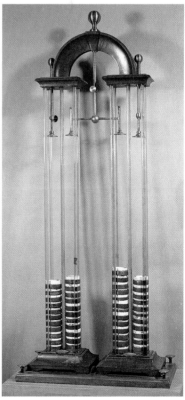

CHARGE IT *At top, an illustration from a book by the Italian physician Luigi Galvani shows him conducting his experiments of 1791 in which he discovered that an electrical charge will cause the legs of dead frogs to twitch, demonstrating the electrical basis of nerve impulses; at right, a voltaic pile; above, a 19th-century print shows Benjamin Franklin's famous kite expriment, in which he attracted lightning to a metal key sent aloft into the sky, proving that lightning was a form of electricity.*

Thomas Hobbes Warns That Life Can Be "Nasty, Brutish, and Short"

46 The mordant British philosopher Thomas Hobbes (1588–1679) lived in a time when the physical sciences had begun to enjoy a newfound prestige. Sir Isaac Newton was discovering laws of motion and gravity that appeared to explain the physical world. Hobbes wished to do something similar in the realm of political theory—to discover the laws that guided the actions of mankind in society. In his powerful appraisal of the human condition, *Leviathan,* published in 1651, he arrived at a very pessimistic view of what those laws might be. Hobbes was writing during the English Civil War, a struggle in which he sided with King Charles I against Parliament and the forces led by Oliver Cromwell. The turmoil added to his dark outlook.

In his book he proposed that in their natural state men— and it's men he speaks about—live in a world of constant struggle and warfare. "If any two men desire the same thing, which nevertheless they cannot both enjoy, they become enemies." What they require is "a common power to keep them all in awe." Without this, he tells us, it's a "war of every man against every man," and in that world human life is, in one of the most famous phrases in all of political thought, "solitary, poor, nasty, brutish, and short."

So given humanity's fang-bearing instincts, what form of social organization does Hobbes suppose it requires for its own safety and survival? He thinks of society as a common-wealth that people form by mutual agreement, what we call a social contract. This commonwealth is the Leviathan, a sort of giant social organism created when individuals come together to achieve the shared goals of safety and security. But that goal can be accomplished only if the community submits to the ab-solute authority of a powerful sovereign. This can be a king— his own preference—or a legislature, as long as the power of the sovereign is supreme and unquestioned. In effect, Hobbes tells us, to be free from chaos, people must put themselves in a sort of prison of their own construction.

BIG IDEA *On the frontispiece of the 1651 edition of* Leviathan, *a giant sym-bolizes Hobbes' notion of a commonwealth ruled by a supreme sovereign.*

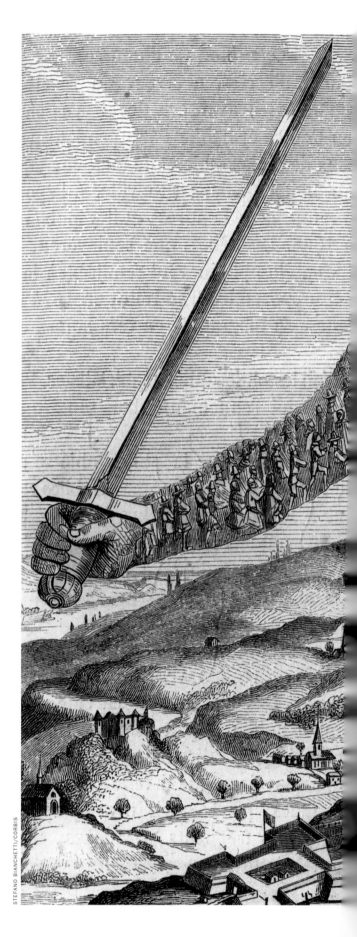

Isaac Newton Deciphers the Rules of the Physical Universe

47 The most important distinguishing characteristic of the Age of Enlightenment—the 17th and 18th centuries—is the rise of science. And the culminating figure of that development is the English mathematician and scientist Sir Isaac Newton (1642–1727). The poet Alexander Pope summed up his era's view of the man in a famous couplet: "Nature and Nature's laws lay hid in night./God said 'Let Newton be!' and all was light."

By close observation and applied mathematics, Newton upended many groundless beliefs that had prevailed for centuries. The ancient Greeks, and all those in later centuries who looked to them, believed that inanimate objects could not move on their own, and so the movement of the moon and planets implied that they were gods, or else moved by gods—or God, as Aristotle put it. Newton, who was deeply religious, though in an unorthodox way, held that God had set the spheres in motion but that once that was done, nothing more was required to keep them moving. He knew this because he had worked out his first law of motion, that a body in motion will tend to remain in motion unless acted upon by an outside force.

Building upon the work of Galileo and Johannes Kepler, Newton developed his greatest achievement, his universal law of gravity. It states that every physical body attracts every other with a force directly proportional to the product of their masses and inversely proportional to the square of the distance between them. That law made it possible for him to explain the movements of the moon and all the planets, the orbits of comets and even the tides. But he did more. He discovered that light was composed of the full spectrum of colors. He perfected a version of the reflecting telescope. He invented calculus. (So did the German mathematician Gottfried Wilhelm von Leibniz, working at roughly the same time, but separately.) Hugely influential, Newton was more than simply a man of science. He was the very idea of science personified.

FAR SEEING *Above, a telescope from 1671 that belonged to Newton; Newton, below, was also deeply interested in theology, but became convinced that the Christian churches of his time had departed from the teachings of Christ.*

Locke and the Social Contract

48 The Enlightenment was not merely a great age of scientific discovery. It was also a great age of social theorizing, as thinkers tried to discover the best ways to organize society. One of the most significant contributions to that effort is the *Two Treatises of Government*, published in 1690 by John Locke (1632–1704). A man of wide interests and exceptional intellect, Locke also produced a highly influential theory of knowledge, based on the idea that all knowledge is derived from experience of the external world obtained through the senses, a view that would come to be known as empiricism.

The *Treatises*, meanwhile, are a classic elaboration of relations between free people and their government and an important contribution to social contract theory—the idea that to gain safety and security for themselves and their property, people willingly cede some of their rights to government. But unlike Thomas Hobbes, Locke believes people retain certain rights that governments must respect. A legitimate government is one that preserves the rights to life, liberty, and property and punishes citizens who violate the rights of others. Among their many legacies, Locke's *Treatises* would be crucial to the thinking behind the American Revolution.

WORLD RENOWN *A French portrait of Locke from 1754*

Vico Develops a Novel Theory of Historical Cycles

49 What is human history? Is it simply one thing after another, with no pattern or meaning? Is it a progress toward a final catastrophic conclusion, as in the apocalyptic endings imagined by many religions? Is it a progress upward toward an ever more just and enlightened arrangement of society? Or is it a cycle that repeats itself again and again? Among the thinkers who have held to the last view, one of the most interesting and influential was a professor of rhetoric at the University of Naples, Giambattista Vico (1668–1744). Vico was also a philosopher whose 1725 book, *The New Science*, put forward a theory of history that depends heavily on a view of how people at different times comprehended their world. Vico saw all societies moving through three distinct stages—the eras of gods, heroes, and men. In his model the ages of gods and heroes were brought forth by creative acts of "imagination." Society emerges first from sense experience and pure feeling, the moment when people invent poetic means (fables and myths) to explain the world. By comparison, the age of men is a more rational era of reflection and philosophy. Reason becomes ascendant and produces civil institutions and other instruments of civilization. Yet while societies strive for perfection, they cannot achieve it, and eventually they return to the practices and understandings of the earliest stage, though at a higher level. The cycle begins again.

Vico's theories of knowledge—that it comes not just from sense experience but from understandings based upon tacit beliefs that emerge out of our experience within our own culture—have intrigued thinkers from Karl Marx to 21st-century structuralists and cultural anthropologists. His work strongly influenced James Joyce as he was writing *Finnegan's Wake*. Even in old age, when Joyce was nearly blind, he hired an Italian to read to him aloud from *The New Science*.

Deism Proposes a God Who Stands Aloof From His World

50 The 18th century was the moment for a short-lived but very influential development in religious thinking—Deism, the belief that God created the world but does not intervene in its affairs, change the course of history, speak from a burning bush, or present himself in any way to the human race he has created. Though they were believers, Deists were opposed to sectarian faith and rejected all institutional religion. That helped ensure that their own brand of faith would be brief, since it had no institutional structure to sustain it. But it was influential because it attacted some of the most prominent men of its time, including Thomas Jefferson, John Adams, James Madison, whose opposition to established religion in the U.S. was based in Deist principles, and the English-born American patriot Thomas Paine. In his book *The Age of Reason*, Paine presented the classic line of Deist thought when he wrote, "I totally disbelieve that the Almighty ever did communicate anything to man, by any mode of speech, in any language, or by any kind of vision or appearance, or by any means which our senses are capable of receiving."

Deism was also the faith of one of the most prominent writers of the 18th century, Francois-Marie Arouet, better known by his pen name, Voltaire (1694–1778). Though he was not a highly original philosopher, Voltaire was the great polemicist of the Enlightenment, the man whose witty and widely read books and essays took up with passion the cause of reason and the fight against superstition. It is Voltaire's antisectarian Deism you hear in the "Prayer to God" he appended to the "Treatise on Tolerance" he published in 1763. There he addresses himself to a "God of all beings, of all worlds, and of all ages."

VOLTAIRE *The French writer and Deist, seen here in one of the several versions of him sculpted by Jean-Antoine Houdon*

LEIBNIZ *Best known to many through Voltaire's parody*

The Best of All Possible Worlds

51 The majestically named Gottfried Wilhelm von Leibniz (1646–1716) was a tremendous figure in 18th-century thought. He made significant contributions to formal logic and binary numbers, the 1 and 0 system used by modern computers. He also invented calculus around the same time as Sir Isaac Newton. But it's been his misfortune to be identified in most people's minds with a single and much scoffed-at doctrine—that we live in the best of all possible worlds: Because God is all powerful, Leibniz reasoned, he could have created any number of alternative universes. Because he is all good, the universe he chose to create must be the best of all the alternatives.

His idea might have sunk into obscurity but for one thing: It infuriated the French *philosophe* Voltaire, who found it absurd, especially in light of the suffering caused by the Lisbon earthquake of 1755, an event that weighed heavily on Voltaire's mind. So Voltaire made Leibniz the recognizable basis for the ridiculous character of Doctor Pangloss in his satirical novel *Candide*, a book that became a classic. Then, in 1956, the composer Leonard Bernstein turned *Candide* into a popular comic operetta, ensuring that future generations will encounter Leibniz as Pangloss, drilling his students in nonsense like this: "Though war may seem a bloody curse / It is a blessing in reverse. / When cannon roar / Both rich and poor / By danger are united! / And every wrong is righted!"

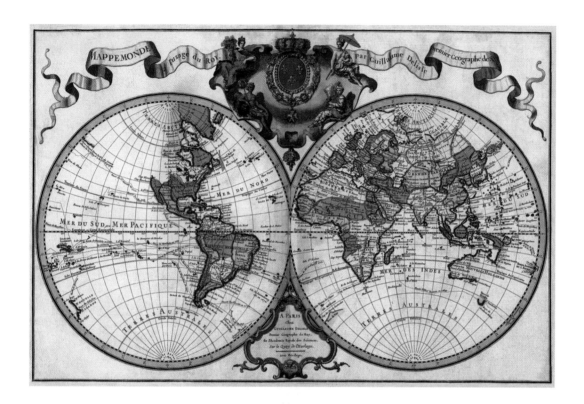

A Skilled Clockmaker Solves a Serious Problem for Navigators

52 Sometimes it takes a carpenter to hammer out a solution to a problem that has stumped the world's greatest scientists. That's the story of longitude. Sailors at sea had long known how to find their latitude, the parallel lines that run east and west on a globe, by gauging the position of the sun and stars over the horizon. But for centuries there was no reliable method to establish longitude, or location with respect to the north-south lines—and that led to shipwrecks and lost vessels. Scientists as prominent as Galileo and Newton had hoped in vain to find a celestial solution, some way to use the stars or moon or even the moons of Jupiter as guideposts. In 1714 an exasperated British government offered 20,000 pounds, more than $12 million today, to anyone who could figure out what to do.

The answer came from John Harrison, an English carpenter and self-taught clockmaker. Harrison's idea, first suggested in the 16th century, involved a shipboard clock set to the hour at zero degree longitude in Greenwich, England. Once at sea, a ship's captain could compare the time on this clock to a second clock set to tell the time at whatever position the ship occupied at that moment. For every hour of difference between the two times, the captain would know that his ship had moved 15 degrees of longitude from zero. The catch was that nothing close to a foolproof clock existed for ocean travel, where the rocking waves played havoc with pendulums, and weather warped delicate clockworks. It was Harrison who designed and built that clock, a process that took decades, working all the while in the face of opposition from men of science convinced that the stars held the answer. In the end he proved that great minds can be found at all levels of society.

ALL AT SEA *Harrison's remarkable marine timekeeper, seen at right in the first of its three versions, from 1735, finally made it possible for oceangoing vessels to plot their longitude. Above, an early-18th-century map displays lines of latitude and longitude.*

MONTESQUIEU *His three-part model of government was designed to prevent any one from prevailing over the others.*

Political Thinkers Propose Dividing the Immense Powers of Government

53 The many examples of unchecked power among European monarchs in the 17th and 18th centuries gave a new urgency to the need to define the necessary elements of a more just and democratic arrangement of government. What was the best way to establish restraints on the power of a leader while at the same time ensuring that citizen majorities didn't exercise unchecked power themselves?

The most widely applied solution came from the French jurist Charles-Louis de Secondat, better known as the Baron de Montesquieu (1689–1755). In *The Spirit of Laws*, published in 1748, he developed the idea of the separation of powers, a notion with sources as far back as ancient Greece. In his *Second Treatise of Government*, the English philosopher John Locke had proposed a two-part government consisting of an executive and a legislature. To that, Montesquieu added the idea of a third branch, the courts. Each branch would exercise "checks and balances" on the other two, ensuring that none of the three would exercise runaway authority.

It was Montesquieu's three-part model of government that was adopted by the framers of the U. S. Constitution. Thus, the President names members of the Supreme Court, but his nominees must be approved by a majority of the Senate. Meanwhile the justices serve for life and have the power to invalidate presidential actions and laws passed by Congress. Presidents can veto laws passed by Congress, which in turn can override the veto, but only with a two-thirds majority vote. For its part, Congress has the power to impeach the President or to investigate members of the executive branch. From the time the Constitution was ratified in 1788, it's been the ceaseless rustling of those "branches" that has produced much of American political life.

THE SIMPLE LIFE *Inspired by Rousseau, French Queen Marie-Antoinette built at Versailles a little dairy farm (above) called the Hameau, where she and her friends could play at being farmers and milkmaids.*

Rousseau Concludes That Man Is Corrupted by Civilization

54 Of all the *philosophes* whose work laid the intellectual foundations of the French Revolution, none was more influential than Swiss-born Jean-Jacques Rousseau (1712–78). In particular his ideas about the essential goodness of human nature captivated late-18th-century Europe. English political thinkers had argued that in "the state of nature"—a world without the institutions of society and government—people would be avaricious, greedy, and violent. In his *Discourse on the Origin of Inequality*, Rousseau proposed instead that people were basically good. It was the institutions of society that had corrupted them over the centuries. In this work he introduced his notion of the "noble savage"—the simple, virtuous man or woman unspoiled by civilization.

Rousseau opened his next work with the famous words: "Man was born free, and he is everywhere in chains." *The Social Contract*, as the book is called, introduced his idea of the general will—something that might be thought of as the combined will of all members of society to achieve the common good. Because he believed that individuals had to submit their own self-interest to the general will, his readers have argued ever since about whether Rousseau opens the way to a tyranny of the majority. Certainly in the darkest moments of the French Revolution, the revolutionary leadership interpreted the general will as a license for terror and dictatorship. So perhaps it's fortunate that Rousseau did not live to see the revolution his work had done so much to bring about.

A Scottish Economist Defines Capitalism

55 By the late 18th century, England was exploding. The bustling port of London was the busiest in the world. In the textile mills of England's northern cities—history's first factories—the first stirrings of the Industrial Revolution were being felt. Improvements in fertilizers and farm implements had led to increased agricultural productivity, which meant that farm families had extra money to spend on those newly manufactured goods. With good reason, England proclaimed itself the "workshop to the world." Taken together, these developments announced a revolution, one that would move outward to transform the world: the emergence of free-market capitalism. One of the first to grasp the dimensions of that change and attempt a lucid account of the foundations of market economies was a professor at the University of Edinburgh, Adam Smith (1723–90). In 1776, the same year Britain's American colonies declared their independence in a dispute that grew largely out of economic grievances, he published the book we know as *Wealth of Nations*, the first work of modern economics.

THE GREAT PORT *In a late-18th-century oil painting, sailing vessels throng the Pool of London, a stretch of the Thames where cargo ships docked.*

At a time when a nation's wealth was commonly reckoned to rest upon the value of its lands or perhaps the gold in its vaults, Smith explained that its wealth in fact derived from the productivity of its people. The more productive they were, the wealthier they would be. But Smith also saw this new market economy in moral terms. All people need the assistance of other people to survive and thrive. What's the best instrument to promote that mutual aid? Smith believed it was business. It's for reasons of self-interest that people work, but through their simultaneous, self-interested enterprise, he believed, they benefit one another. It was in this book that Smith advanced his famous idea of the "invisible hand" of the market, which directs self-interested economic actions to aid the common good, regardless of the fact that the individuals performing those actions intend to help only themselves.

At the same time, Smith understood the difference between beneficial self-interest and harmful greed. He recognized that manufacturers and other producers were likely to use methods like monopolies, trade barriers, and price-fixing to artificially increase prices and profits. It was the role of government, he believed, to curb those abuses—in effect, to keep free markets free.

Kant Delves Deep Into the Mind and Morality

56 Immanuel Kant (1724–1804) was born in the Prussian city of Königsberg and never in his life traveled more than 50 miles from it. He attended the University of Königsberg and then spent four decades there as a tutor and lecturer. But from within his tightly circumscribed personal world he launched what he rightly described as a "Copernican revolution in philosophy" that made him one of the most important figures in the history of Western thought. In his *Critique of Pure Reason,* he explored the question of what things the mind can know and how it knows them, examining the ways in which reason not only creates the conditions from which knowledge emerges but also places limits on what we can know. In *Critique of Practical Reason*, an inquiry into the foundations of morality, Kant developed his influential idea of "categorical imperatives"—actions that we must perform because they are moral obligations, regardless of our personal motives or inclinations. The only truly moral actions are those we undertake for reasons that could be universal laws for all people. Put another way, it's wrong to allow yourself to act in one way if you would want other people to act differently. So it's wrong to steal if you can't reasonably want to make theft a universal possibility for everyone else. For all his renown, to this day Kant has never left Königsberg, now the Russian city of Kaliningrad. He's buried in a mausoleum adjoining its cathedral.

Hegel Outlines the Dialectic

HEGEL *"Every individual being," he once wrote, "is some one aspect of the Idea."*

57 To the German philosopher Georg Wilhelm Friedrich Hegel (1770–1831), ultimate truth —or what he called "absolute spirit"—is literally a work in progress. It unfolds over time through the history of philosophy and the contest of ideas. Using an ancient Greek term, Hegel called this process a "dialectic." It begins with an idea he called a "thesis." Eventually the thesis gives rise to its opposite, a contradictory idea that has an equal claim to validity. This he calls the "antithesis." Eventually the conflicting ideas are reconciled in what he calls the "synthesis," which itself becomes the next thesis, so that the process begins anew. Through these slow workings of human thought, absolute spirit—a notion that he defined in very complex terms—is effectively creating itself. He also believed that history was itself a dialectical unfolding of the same absolute spirit, or as he sometimes called it, absolute idea. In Hegel's description, "History is Mind clothing itself with the form of events."

The greatest impact of Hegel's thinking outside the world of philosophy would come when the dialectic was adapted by Karl Marx, who took it out of the realm of pure thought. It became important to his idea of "historical materialism," in which history progresses in stages determined by ownership of the means of production. At each stage contradictions arise in a process that produces struggles that result in the next stage. In that way, he believed, feudalism gave rise to capitalism, which in turn produced contradictions that would give rise to communism, which he thought would be the final stage of history. About that, it certainly appears, he was wrong.

CHAOS THEORY *It was the turmoil of the French Revolution, seen here in an image of the storming of the Bastille, that inspired Burke's* Reflections.

Edmund Burke Defines the Idea of Conservatism

58 The French Revolution began in 1789 as an uprising of the poor and the emerging middle classes against an oppressive aristocratic society. Within a few years it would devolve into the despotism and bloodshed of the Reign of Terror. Long before the Terror got underway, the Irish-born British statesman and thinker Edmund Burke (1729–1797) was already deeply apprehensive about the premises on which the revolution rested and the course it was likely to take. In November 1790, just 16 months after the storming of the Bastille, Burke would publish *Reflections on the Revolution in France*, a classic defense of traditional institutions, social order, and evolutionary change. It would become one of the foundational texts of modern conservative thought.

What troubled Burke about the revolution was that it represented a massive social experiment, one that presumed to start society over from scratch on the basis of rational principles. He believed it was dangerous to uproot institutions wholesale. "Good order is the foundation of all things," he wrote. He was also skeptical about how much of a role reason really plays in human affairs and decision-making. He believed things like custom, faith, and even prejudice play a large and necessary part. He also valued local communities and small-scale associations as the basic fabric of society and was suspicious of the centralized state. Above all, historical continuity was crucial to him. Society cannot be upended at will, he believed, because the present is a "partnership between those who are living, those who are dead, and those who are yet to be born."

A Remarkable Woman Calls for Women's Rights

59 The thinkers of the Enlightenment spoke regularly and eloquently about the rights of man. But when they did, they often seemed to have only men in mind. It was not until 1792 that someone stepped forward to speak at length about conditions endured by the other half of the human race. That was the year Mary Wollstonecraft (1759–97) published *A Vindication of the Rights of Woman*. A former teacher and governess, Wollstonecraft identified the failure to educate women for any independent role in life as the great source of their difficulties. Men led women to be "docile and attentive to their looks to the exclusion of all else," she wrote. She called marriage "legal prostitution" and demanded the vote, proclaiming, "Let woman share the rights and she will emulate the virtues of man."

Wollstonecraft was just 38 when she died, a few days after giving birth to a daughter, Mary (later the wife of the poet Percy Bysshe Shelley and the author of *Frankenstein)*. After Wollstonecraft's death, her husband, the political philosopher William Godwin, published a biography of his wife that frankly acknowledged her early affair with an American lover and the illegitimate child she bore him. Opponents soon used those revelations to dismiss her. But her arguments would inspire later generations, including the suffragists, who brought women the vote, and the feminist activists of the 1960s and '70s.

All Men Are Created Equal

60 "We hold these truths to be self-evident, that all men are created equal ..." Those powerful words from the all-important second paragraph of the Declaration of Independence, represented a watershed in the life of an idea that had sources going back as far as the ancient world and the precepts of Jesus Christ. But it required centuries of struggle for it to find genuine and widespread acceptance. It was Thomas Jefferson (1743–1826) who composed the words, which were then amended by Benjamin Franklin. Jefferson had originally described the truths as "sacred and undeniable," effectively rooting them in religious traditions. Franklin made them "self-evident," basing them in traditions of reason going back to the self-evident axioms of the ancient Greek mathematician Euclid and the "analytic truths" of Franklin's close friend, the eminent Scottish philosopher David Hume.

Despite the confident tone of the famous assertion, equality was not an idea that would have seemed "self-evident" in most cultures and times—or even at the time and in the place the words were written. It's a well-recognized irony of the Declaration that fully a third of the 56 men who signed it in July 1776 were slaveholders, including Jefferson, and few of them would have agreed that their black slaves were their equals. Real equality for women was also unimaginable to most men of the time. So it would be a long journey before that phrase took on real substance, one that would require a civil war and a century of turmoil after that. Yet with that momentous document the journey had truly begun.

HER LEGACY *Suffragists active in the movement to obtain the vote for women, like these on parade in New York City in 1919, often repeated arguments advanced by Wollstonecraft.*

WORTH REPEATING *The Declaration's language about equality would find its way into other documents, including the Massachusetts Constitution of 1780, written largely by John Adams.*

81

CHURCH & STATE

The U.S. Pioneers a Lasting Separation of Church and State

61 Church and state have struggled to establish their proper relationship virtually since religion and government first developed. Egyptian pharaohs were held to be descendents of gods. At various times Roman and Japanese emperors were treated as gods themselves. Every Holy Roman Emperor from Charlemagne through Charles V in 1530 was crowned by the pope. And in much of the world there are still state religions or established churches, like Britain's Church of England.

In the 18th century there would be two notable attempts to remove religion from the realm of government authority. In France, where Catholicism had long been the established faith, the revolutionary governments that emerged after 1789 abolished its privileges. But Napoleon reestablished the Church's preeminence in 1801, a status it sustained until 1905. It was the U.S. that undertook the more enduring effort to solve the question with the First Amendment to the Constitution, adopted as part of the Bill of Rights in 1791. "Congress shall make no law respecting an establishment of religion, or prohibiting the free exercise thereof"—with those words the founders laid the basis for what Thomas Jefferson would later call the "wall of separation" between church and state. Just exactly what the amendment requires or prohibits remains a topic of intense debate, but for more than two centuries it has ensured that Americans can freely practice any faith or none.

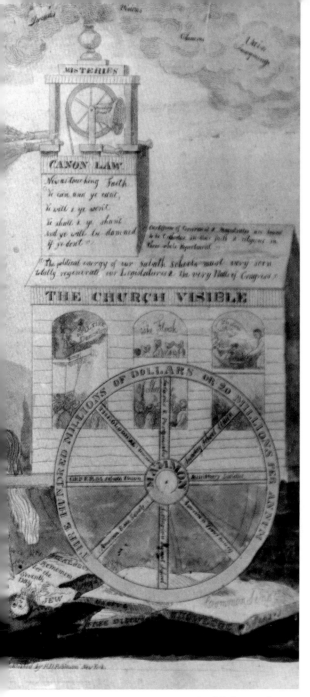

THE LETTERS OF THE LAW *A political cartoon from around 1816 satirizes attempts by Christian organizations to prevent the United States Postal Service from delivering mail on Sundays.*

Utilitarians Seek the Greatest Happiness for All

62 Utilitarianism, a school of thought that emerged in England in the late 18th century and flourished in the one that followed, rests on one of the most agreeable-sounding premises in the history of philosophy: the "greatest-happiness principle." It had its beginnings in the work of Jeremy Bentham (1748–1832), the son of a wealthy London family who trained as a lawyer but never practiced, deciding instead to devote himself to the life of a thinker. Borrowing from the ancient Greek Epicureans, Bentham arrived at his "principle of utility," that the chief aim of life is to attain pleasure and avoid pain. As he wrote, "They govern us in all we do, in all we say, in all we think."

From that it followed that the first rule of living should be to maximize pleasure and minimize pain. Further, the laws and institutions of society should be designed to accomplish that goal wherever possible for the greatest number of people. Bentham even developed a "felicific calculus"—a way to determine the precise amount of pleasure that any particular action might produce.

One of Bentham's chief disciples was the philosopher James Mill, whose son John Stuart Mill (1806–73) became the next major figure in the development of utilitarianism. It was the younger Mill who actually coined the phrase "greatest-happiness principle." But Mill departed from Bentham in a few important ways. For one, Bentham treated all pleasures as essentially equal. In a famous example, he proposed that if hopscotch gave more people pleasure than opera, then society should devote more resources to promoting hopscotch. Mill distinguished between what he termed higher and lower pleasures, and judged intellectual and moral pleasures to be superior to merely physical ones. As he put it, "It is better to be a human being dissatisfied than a pig satisfied; better to be Socrates dissatisfied than a fool satisfied."

In our own time, though we may not call ourselves utilitarians, the assumption that the best actions are the ones that produce the greatest happiness informs many of our judgments about laws and social policies.

STARRY NIGHT *An image taken by NASA's Hubble Space Telescope shows clouds of interstellar dust swirling around a distant star*

Modern Times

Romanticism Gives Vent to the Passions

63 It was probably inevitable that the Enlightenment, a period that worshipped cool reason, would give rise to a backlash, a period that cherished feeling, sentiment, and hot passion. We call that enduring development romanticism, and from the late 18th century through much of the 19th it swept Europe and the U.S. Romanticism transformed every area of cultural life—fiction, poetry, drama, art, and music—in ways we still live with. English poets like William Wordsworth, Samuel Taylor Coleridge, and John Keats composed paeans to the natural world and to romantic solitude. ("My imagination is a monastery," wrote Keats, "and I am its monk.") Instead of looking to the Classical past, romantics indulged a fascination for the Middle Ages. One result was the "gothic" novel, works like *The Castle of Otranto* by Horace Walpole, which virtually invented the apparatus of modern horror—monsters, ghosts, old castles, and stormy nights. Another was the invention of historical fiction by Sir Walter Scott, whose novels recreated a lost world of medieval England.

Politics would also be strongly infected by the romantic embrace of nationalist passion and its idealization of folklore and folk traditions, which helped drive the struggle for unification in Italy and Germany. And on the individual plane, the brooding solitary soul became the romantic ideal. Poets such as Lord Byron—whom Lady Caroline Lamb called "mad, bad, and dangerous to know"—became the spiritual ancestor of every Hollywood rebel from James Dean to Johnny Depp.

LOST IN THOUGHT The Wanderer Above the Sea of Fog, *from 1818, by romantic painter Caspar David Friedrich*

Transcendentalism Decries the Bustle of American Life

64 Though its population was still predominantly rural, by the 1830s the U.S. was on its way to becoming the economic dynamo it was fated to be. It was at this moment that a few notable men and women converged to bemoan the materialism and conformity of their fellow citizens and to preach a nondenominational spirituality to be achieved through "intuition" rather than religious dogmas, one that sought to "transcend" the merely physical world. Their message had sources in German idealist philosophy and English romanticism, as well as the Vedas, the ancient sacred texts of the Hindu religion. It was largely a New England phenomenon, centered near Concord, Mass., the home of its central figure, the essayist and lecturer Ralph Waldo Emerson (1803–82), an oracular and subtle thinker who denounced a modern world that offered "a life without love, and an activity without an aim."

RALPH WALDO EMERSON *The eminent American essayist as he appeared around 1860*

Like the English romantics, Emerson loved nature. ("In the woods," he wrote, "is perpetual youth.") So did his friend Henry David Thoreau (1817–62), who in 1854 published *Walden.* An account of his two years spent living in a woodland cabin near Concord, the book is a classic meditation on self-sufficiency, nature, and the pitfalls of worldly ambition. "Why should we be in such desperate haste to succeed?" he asked. "If a man does not keep pace with his companions, perhaps it is because he hears a different drummer."

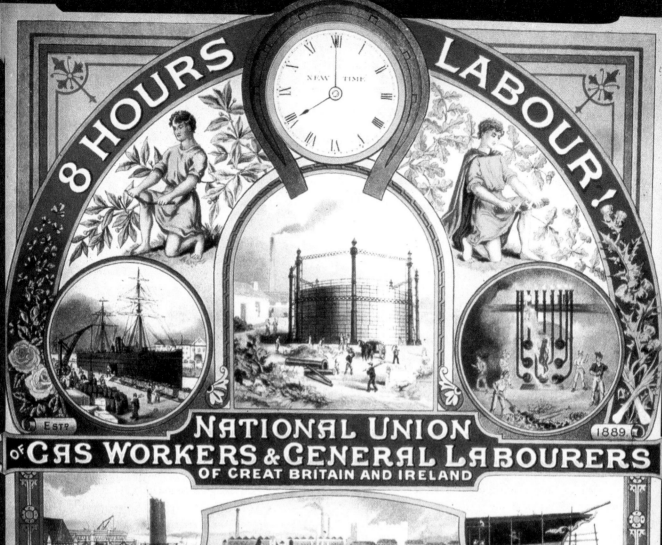

8 HOURS

NEW TIME

LABOUR!

NATIONAL UNION
OF GAS WORKERS & GENERAL LABOURERS
OF GREAT BRITAIN AND IRELAND

ESTD

1889.

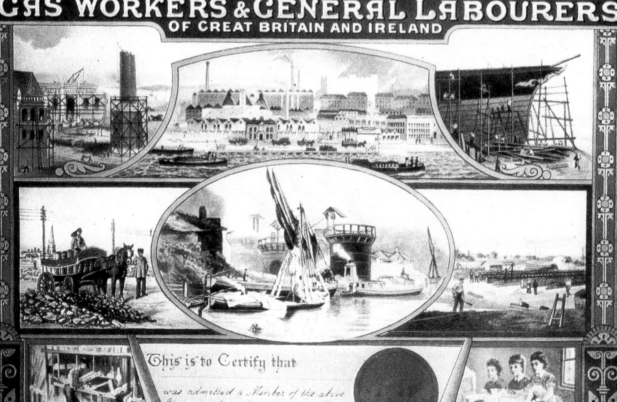

This is to Certify that

was admitted a Member of the above
Union on the   of day of   18

Secretary

Laborers Unite for Better Pay and Working Conditions

65 The industrial revolution that got underway in late-18th-century England soon spread across Europe and then to the U.S. The new factory economy utterly transformed the social structure of every nation where it emerged. It gave rise to the industrial working class: men, women, and even children who toiled for long hours for low pay in a world in which the factory, mill, and mine owners held all the cards. It was a world without rules to require safe workplaces, without limits on the length of the workday, without minimum-wage laws, health benefits, or prohibitions on child labor. Faced with those circumstances, it was only a matter of time before workers arrived at the idea of banding together to counteract the power of the owners. But in England the first unions, or "combinations," as they were also called, were quickly declared illegal by the Combination Acts of 1799 and 1800. They were legalized at last in 1824, though even 10 years later, six English farm workers, the "Tolpuddle martyrs," could still be convicted of "illegal oath-taking"—in other words, joining a union—and transported to Australia.

In the U.S. printers were the first trade to go on strike, in New York in 1794; cabinetmakers two years later, carpenters in Philadelphia the year after that. But the great industrial leap forward for the U.S. truly got underway in the 1830s, and the number of unions grew, especially after the Civil War. The National Labor Union, a federation of local unions, emerged in 1866. Though it lasted less than a decade, it persuaded Congress to require a maximum eight-hour workday for federal workers. A more enduring organization was the American Federation of Labor, founded in 1886 by Samuel Gompers, a Jewish immigrant from Britain. "Show me the country that has no strikes," he once said, "and I'll show you the country that has no liberty."

WELCOME TO THE CLUB *This membership certificate from 1889 certifies that the holder belongs to the Anglo-Irish trade union that successfully pushed for an eight-hour workday.*

FIRESTORM *A 19th-century engraving depicts the chaotic gunfire during Chicago's Haymarket Square Tragedy of May 4, 1886.*

Anarchists Envision an Orderly World Without Government

66 While the 17th and 18th centuries were the great period for theories of government, the 19th put forward a theory of antigovernment. Anarchism envisioned a world order resting upon a fabric of voluntary associations of all sizes, one that would make the evils of government unnecessary. As Prince Peter Kropotkin (1842–1921) expressed it in his 1896 book, *Anarchism: Its Philosophy and Ideal,* "When we ask for the abolition of the state and its organs, we are always told that we dream of a society composed of men better than they are in reality. But no; a thousand times, no. All we ask is that men should not be made worse than they are, by such institutions." Though there are stirrings of anarchist thought in earlier centuries, the first writer to use the term was the French political thinker Pierre-Joseph Proudhon (1809–65), who famously declared in his 1840 book, *What is Property?,* that "property is theft!"

Anarchists were important to the struggle against fascism during the Spanish Civil War. But the movement was also hurt by its association with terrorist violence. In 1886 four anarchists were convicted after Chicago's Haymarket Square Tragedy, which occurred when an unknown person threw a bomb at police officers, attempting to break up a peaceful demonstration. Between 1894 and 1901 alone, anarchists killed the President of France, the Prime Minister of Spain, Empress Elizabeth of Austria, King Umberto I of Italy, and U.S. President William McKinley—acts that brought to anarchism the taint of anarchy.

FIRST IMPRESSIONS *Clockwise from top: An 1839 self-portrait by Philadelphia photographer Robert Cornelius is among the earliest photo portraits; Fox Talbot's 1839 nature study is one of the first images made using his paper process; Timothy H. O'Sullivan's 1864 picture of Union soldiers is an example of documentary photography; in 1843 the British eye doctor Jabez Hogg uses a watch to time a daguerreotype exposure.*

Photography Ignites a Visual Revolution

67 No one can put a date on the cave drawings at Lascaux or on the first drumbeat. But photography has a birthdate of sorts, 1839, the year it was ushered loudly into the world in a clamor of patents and the claims of two inventors, Louis-Jacques-Mandé Daguerre in France and William Henry Fox Talbot in England. Daguerre improved upon discoveries made earlier by Joseph Niépce, a retired French army officer who had found a way to fix images on a pewter plate covered with bitumen, a material that reacted to light. Fox Talbot's method involved exposing the image on treated paper. Daguerreotypes achieved higher detail, but each was one of a kind. Fox Talbot's technique produced an unlimited number of prints from a single negative.

In the mid-19th century the modern world was taking shape—in some respects the shape that photography gave it. The new art form fostered the trend by which the ancient notion of fame was supplanted by the more salable idea of celebrity. And in the great age of imperial expansion, the camera proved just the tool to bring home views of the exotic places the Western powers had subjugated. By the early 1840s the world's first portrait studios had sprung up in New York City and Philadelphia, churning out likenesses of glassy-eyed sitters who looked as though they had been whacked with a board—a consequence of the long period they had to remain perfectly still before the lens. But it was in England and France that photography took on the character of art in the work of men like the Parisian caricaturist Nadar, who brought a warm-blooded gravity to camera portraiture.

The camera remained for decades an exotic box, a contraption mostly for adventurers and the wealthy. That changed after 1888, the year George Eastman introduced the inexpensive Kodak. With "snapshots" now a possibility, amateur photography became the new folk art.

KARL MARX *"Workers of the world, unite!" he urged.*

Karl Marx and Friedrich Engels Analyze the Capitalist System

68 For much of the 20th century, the most influential thinker of the 19th was indisputably Karl Marx (1818–83). From 1917, when the Bolsheviks took power in Moscow, until 1989, when jubilant crowds tore down the Berlin Wall, Marxism was the dogma that ruled the lives of millions of people in the Soviet Union and Eastern Europe. Today it remains the basis for the systems of government and economics in Cuba, Laos, North Korea, Vietnam, and even in quasi-capitalist China. As Marx once wrote, "The philosophers have only interpreted the world in various ways; the point, however, is to change it." And change it he did, though not perhaps in ways he intended.

Marx claimed to have put socialism on a "scientific" footing and to have discerned the laws by which history operates. He believed that in his own time the working class held the key to history, which he saw as a struggle between the capitalist owners of the means of production—the bourgeoisie, as he sometimes termed them—and the oppressed workers, the proletariat. Eventually, he predicted, the burgeoning ranks of the proletariat in most nations would revolt, take power in what he termed a "dictatorship of the proletariat," and abolish the capitalist system.

One of the books in which Marx famously laid out that theory was *The Communist Manifesto*, a call to arms he co-authored with his friend and collaborator Friedrich Engels (1820–95) in 1848, which would prove to be a year of widespread revolutionary turmoil, some of it fanned by the new communist parties springing up around Europe. "Let the ruling classes tremble at a communist revolution," the authors declared. "The proletarians have nothing to lose but their chains. They have a world to win."

BIRTH OF A NATION *A 19th-century lithograph shows General Giuseppe Garibaldi entering Naples on Sept. 8, 1860, the year in which he and his volunteer army scored decisive victories in the struggle to create a unified Italy.*

Nationalism Becomes an Ever More Powerful Force

69 Tribal identity may be as old as humanity. But not until the 19th century does the more abstract notion of nationality, of membership in a broad community with shared institutions, traditions, and symbols, get seriously underway. In the late 18th century the poet Johann Gottfried Herder (1744–1803) had developed the notion of *Volksgeist*—national character or spirit— that would be fundamental to national identity in Germany and elsewhere. Soon Napoleon's campaigns gave an enhanced sense of nationhood to the French, while often doing the same for the peoples outside France who fought him. Borne on a wave of nationalist fervor, by the 1870s the modern nations of Italy and Germany had emerged from a patchwork of previously independent principalities and duchies.

The intellectual historian Isaiah Berlin once called nationalism "an inflamed condition of national consciousness." By the later 19th century it had metastasized into the philosophy and practice of imperialism. The European powers competed to divide up Africa. Various parts of Asia fell under the control of Britain, France, Japan, and the U.S. By 1914 roughly four-fifths of the world's land surface was under the control of a handful of nations. To dignify the imperial scramble—and disguise its real motives—those nations embraced the idea of the civilizing mission, the benefits that colonial rule brought to subject peoples. As the British poet Rudyard Kipling put it, "Take up the White Man's burden / ... To serve your captives' need."

FREE AT LAST *A painting by François Auguste Biard depicts the 1848 emancipation of slaves in the French colonies. More than 250,000 were freed, most in the West Indies and Réunion. Though abolished by the French Revolution, slavery had been reinstituted by Napoleon.*

HARRIET TUBMAN *Born into slavery in Maryland around 1820, she conducted many fugitive slaves to freedom in the North.*

The World Gradually Recognizes That Slavery Must Be Outlawed

70 Slavery may have been one of humanity's worst ideas, but it also proved to be difficult to let go of. It began in the earliest moments of history. Slaves are mentioned in the Code of Hammurabi and appear frequently in the Old Testament. They were a foundation of even the most democratic Greek city-states. Ancient China and India, the Islamic caliphates, medieval Europe, and the pre-Columbian civilizations of North and South America—all took slavery for granted.

This state of affairs persisted in Europe until the later Middle Ages, when slavery at last began to disappear in Europe. In Japan it ended in the 16th century. In England, where slavery began to be outlawed as early as the 12th century, there arose a movement in the late 18th to end as well any British participation in the trade that carried African slaves in terrible conditions across the Atlantic to be sold in Britain's colonies. Under the leadership of William Wilberforce (1759–1833), a social reformer and member of Parliament, the trade was banned at last in 1807, and in 1833 slaves in most parts of the British Empire were also declared free. Russia was next. In 1861, Czar Alexander II abolished serfdom in his nation. Though not technically slaves, serfs were peasant farmworkers bound to their master and to his land. It was estimated that by the middle of the 19th century, half of Russia's 40 million peasants were serfs. In the U.S. the end of slavery would require a prolonged civil war. Though President Abraham Lincoln opposed the extension of slavery into territories beyond the Southern and border states where it was legal, in his first inaugural address he pledged not to interfere with slavery in those states. But in January 1863, with the war underway, he issued the Emancipation Proclamation, an executive order that freed 3.1 million of the nation's 4 million slaves. In 1865, after the Union victory over the Confederate South, slavery was officially banned by the 13th amendment to the U.S. Constitution.

A Scientific Monk Discovers the Rules of Genetics

71 Long before they understood its mechanisms, human beings had some grasp of genetics, the science of heredity. As early as 5000 B.C., cultures around the world were crossbreeding livestock as well as such crops as wheat, corn, rice, and dates to produce superior new varieties. But an understanding of those mechanisms began only in the 19th century, in the work of Gregor Mendel (1822–84), a Catholic monk and natural history teacher living in what is now the Czech city of Brno. He conducted his studies in the simplest imaginable laboratory—the garden of his Augustinian monastery, where he grew peas. Between 1856 and 1863, Mendel observed the ways in which traits like height, color, and wrinkled surface were passed from one generation of plants to the next. What he discovered is that most such traits are carried by what we now call genes. He also determined that genes can be dominant or recessive. For example, when red-flowered peas are crossed with white-flowered peas, all the seeds grow into plants with red flowers—the red-flower gene is dominant. But when those red hybrids are crossed with each other, one fourth of the next generation is white—the white-flower gene is recessive.

In 1866, Mendel published his findings about patterns of inheritance in a relatively obscure journal, *The Proceedings of the Brünn Society for Natural Science*, where they were largely ignored by the scientific world. Two years later he was made abbot of his monastery and put his scientific work aside. Not until 1900 would his work be rediscovered by botanists, opening the way for a century of work in genetics and leading to the Human Genome Project, the 13-year effort begun in 1990 to identify all of the roughly 25,000 genes in our DNA.

SEEDS OF AN IDEA *At top, Mendel drew his conclusions about heredity by observing how the pink pea flowers at left, when crossed with the white pea flowers at right, produce the hybrid flowers in the middle; above, green and yellow peas of the type Mendel studied.*

The Russian Intelligentsia Descends Into "Nihilism"

72 "A nihilist is a person who does not bow down to any authority, who does not accept any principle on faith, however much that principle may be revered." Those are the words of Arkady Kirsanov, a shy university graduate in *Fathers and Sons*, the great novel from 1862 by the Russian writer Ivan Turgenev. Though the term "nihilism" was first used by the German philosopher Friedrich Heinrich Jacobi in the 18th century, it was Turgenev who popularized it. In the character of Arkady's friend Yevgeny Bazarov, a brusque, cynical young medical student who worships science, sneers at the idea of moral principles, and rejects all institutions, Turgenev created an unforgettable portrait of nihilism's across-the-board repudiation of tradition. In the 1860s nihilism appealed to a generation of young Russian intellectuals struggling to absorb the lessons of the Enlightenment, which had arrived belatedly in their native land in the 19th century. What began as a revolt against religious dogma and czarist absolutism developed over time into the rejection of all forms of belief and authority. Something Bazarov says in Turgenev's novel —"What matters is that twice two makes four, and the rest is all rubbish"—could have served as its motto.

In the decade that followed, nihilism provided a philosophical point of departure for ever more radical and desperate varieties of revolutionary activity in Russia, a period characterized by terrorism and secret societies that culminated in the assassination of Czar Alexander II in 1881. In his 1869 manifesto, *Cathechism of a Revolutionist*, the anarchist Sergei Nechaev could announce that the revolutionary "knows one science only: the science of destruction." Nechaev would be the inspiration for the character of Pyotr Verkhovensky in Fyodor Dostoevsky's novel *The Devils*, also known as *The Possessed*. Verkhovensky leads a secret society that in its ruthlessness and perverse internal dynamics seems to foreshadow both the Baader-Meinhof group—German terrorists whose heyday was the 1970s—and the Manson family.

Charles Darwin Develops the Theory of Evolution

73 It could have been no more than a lark, an upper-class British graduate's equivalent of the grand tour. But naturalist Charles Darwin's five-year voyage on a British cartographic ship, *H.M.S. Beagle*, which he began in 1831 when he was only 22, changed our understanding of human existence. After stops to chart the coast of South America, the *Beagle* explored the Galápagos Islands, an isolated volcanic archipelago straddling the equator. It was there that Darwin noticed that on each island there were identical species of finches whose beaks differed in size and structure. From this observation he later extrapolated his theory of natural selection, the evolutionary process by which organisms with superior adaptive characteristics tend to survive and pass on those qualities. On returning to England he continued his research and in 1859 published his great work: *On the Origin of Species by Means of Natural Selection*.

Darwin's theories proved to be among history's most divisive ideas. Victorians mocked his argument that all species of life descended from common ancestors: Was his grandfather an ape? His arguments that survival favors the fittest spawned a host of bogus theories of eugenics and racial superiority, including those of Adolf Hitler. And because his premises do not posit God's hand in creation, they have been attacked for more than 150 years, most recently by advocates for faith who argue that this world shows all the hallmarks of "intelligent design," i.e., divine creation. Indeed, Darwin's ideas, now overwhelmingly accepted by scientists, helped create an enduring chasm between science and some religions: A 2005 *Time* poll found that 54% of Americans do not believe that human beings evolved from earlier species.

WILLIAM PERLMAN/STAR LEDGER/CORBIS (CENTER);THE BRIDGEMAN ART LIBRARY (2)

FROM TOP LEFT: ENGLISH HERITAGE PHOTO LIBRARY/BRIDGEMAN ART LIBRARY;THE STAPLETON COLLECTION/ BRIDGEMAN ART LIBRARY

THE EVOLUTIONARY *Clockwise from above: a portrait of Darwin by the famed British photographer Julia Margaret Cameron; fish noted by Darwin in his book* The Zoology of the Voyage of the H.M.S Beagle, 1832–36; *in his journal, Darwin mused on the tree of life; a picture of a carrier pigeon from Darwin's home in Kent, where he often studied such birds; a water color depicted the* Beagle *approaching Tierra del Fuego.*

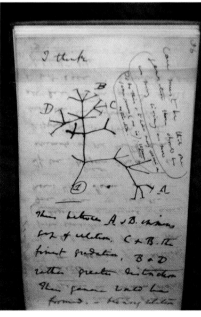

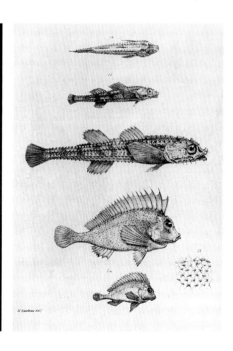

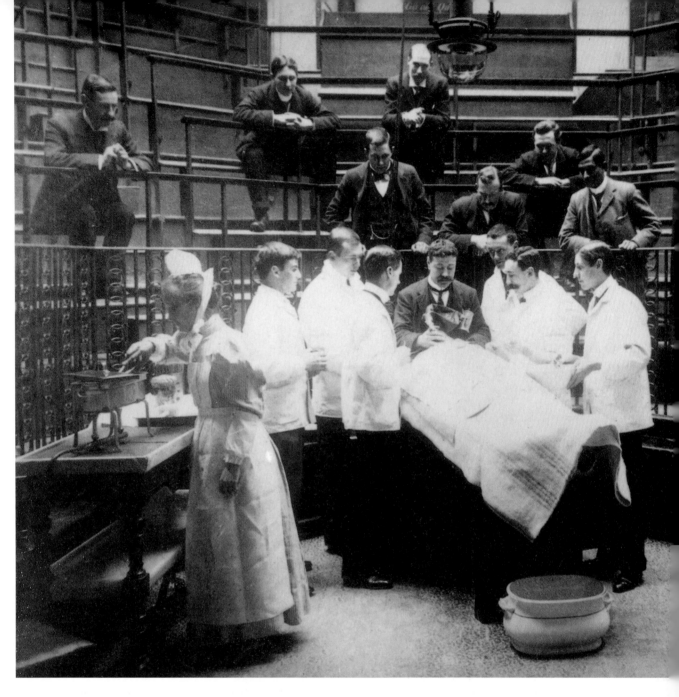

Science Discovers That Germs Are the Cause of Many Diseases

74 | It may be the single most beneficial idea in history—the discovery that microorganisms cause most illnesses. The germ theory of disease enabled medicine at last to develop treatments based on sturdy science. It could be said to have its beginnings in the 1670s, when the Dutch lens grinder Anton van Leeuwenhoek, using a simple microscope, became the first person ever to observe microorganisms. But its two pivotal figures emerged in the 19th century: the French chemist and microbiologist Louis Pasteur (1822–95) and the British surgeon Joseph Lister (1827–1912). In the 1860s, Pasteur conducted experiments on both sealed and unsealed containers of beverages, observing that only the broth in unsealed containers fermented, proving it was infected by airborne agents, in this case spores of yeast. By that means he confirmed the germ theory, which others had earlier proposed. He also refuted the theory of spontaneous generation, a belief dating back to the ancient Greeks that living matter can arise from inanimate matter. In 1864 he also invented the process we call pasteurization—heating beverages like milk and beer to eliminate microorganisms that cause them to spoil—and later he developed the first vaccines.

In the mid 19th century, postoperative infection led to the death of nearly half of all surgical patients. When Lister heard of Pasteur's work, he realized that microbes must be the cause of the infections and devised a way to disinfect surgical incisions using carbolic acid. The age of modern medicine had begun.

THE BATTLE AGAINST INFECTION *In 1898, British medical students observe an operation. A nurse at left tends what appears to be a boiling-water device used to sterilize surgical instruments, one of the germ-killing methods introduced after Lister's discoveries about bacteria.*

FRIEDRICH NIETZSCHE *The philosopher in 1873*

Nietzsche Analyzes Western Culture

75 What nearly everyone knows about the German philosopher Friedrich Nietzsche (1844–1900) is that he declared that God is dead. They also usually know that years after his death his ideas about the will to power and the superman were put to lethal misuse by the Nazis. But his thinking was always more complex than the slogans and misreadings sometimes attached to it. Though he spent some years teaching at the University of Basel, he was too original a mind for academic life. He was trained in philology, the historical study of languages, with a specialization in ancient Greek texts, and his first book, *The Birth of Tragedy*, in 1872, was much more than a meditation on ancient theater. It put forward what would become a very influential idea of two competing impulses in Greek culture that could also be understood as forces shaping the universe generally. One, associated with the god Apollo, represented reason, solid form, and moderation. The other was a wild, instinctual force identified with the god Dionysus. Far from being purely destructive, the Dionysian was something that Nietzsche saw as a healthy creative impulse of which European culture needed more.

A decade later, in his book *The Gay Science*, he would make his claim about the death of God, but he puts the statement in the mouth of a madman, who adds, "and we have killed him." It was Nietzsche's means of saying that God was no longer a moral guidepost that mankind could believe in and live by. How, then, to establish what he would call a "hierarchy of values"? This would remain his lifelong quest, through episodes of ill health and finally madness, a quest he knew would be a tragic one. "If you gaze for long into an abyss," he once wrote, "the abyss also gazes into you."

Pragmatism Declares That Truth Is What Works

76 To the extent that the United States remains a nation that values results over ideology, it seems fitting that one of the most successful schools of thought to come out of the U.S. is called "pragmatism." It was chiefly the product of William James (1842–1910). A professor of psychology at Harvard and the brother of the novelist Henry James, he had a strong interest in philosophy and deeply held religious beliefs. But his central idea, which he put forward in *The Will to Believe* in 1896 and *Pragmatism* in 1907, was in effect a refutation of the importance of belief in the conventional sense. What he proposed instead was that the truth of any idea was a matter of its usefulness. "An idea is 'true,'" James wrote, "so long as to believe it is profitable to our lives."

James subjected his belief in God to his own test. He acknowledged that there is no clear-cut physical evidence that God exists or does not exist. But he felt all the same that it was possible to demonstrate that belief in God has positive benefits on believers. This was something he had already done in his 1902 classic *The Varieties of Religious Experience*, a book based upon a series of lectures he had given at the University of Edinburgh. In it he collected many case studies of people who had found contentment through religion. And so, he concluded, "if the hypothesis of God works satisfactorily in the widest sense of the word, it is true"—a pragmatic conclusion, to be sure, but one that would probably never satisfy more orthodox believers.

SIGMUND FREUD *Hugely influential, but now out of favor*

Sigmund Freud Produces a New Picture of How the Mind Works

77 In the history of Western thought there is no more confounding a figure than Sigmund Freud (1856–1939), the father of psychoanalysis. Ideas he introduced—repressed anxieties, projected desires, defense mechanisms, guilt complexes, ambivalent feelings—have become everyday expressions. His central contention, that many of our behaviors emerge from sources in the unconscious, utterly transformed our picture of ourselves. Yet in the one area for which his theories were developed—the treatment of mental illness—his influence, once immense, is largely finished. In that realm approaches based on behavior therapy and medication have eclipsed Freudian analysis, and Freud's picture of the mind and its workings is sharply contested.

Born in Freiberg in what is now the Czech Republic, Freud was 4 when his family moved to Vienna. He lived there until the Nazis annexed Austria in 1938, and Freud, who was Jewish, fled to England. In Vienna he studied medicine and eventually specialized in the treatment of hysteria, a broad category of disorders that could include everything from mysterious paralysis to simple anxiety and depression. In time he concluded that all hysteria had its source in a childhood sexual experience that the adult had suppressed. His colleague Josef Breuer would break with him over what he considered Freud's excessive focus on sexual trauma as the root of all neurosis. But building upon techniques used by Breuer, Freud developed a method of treatment that involved having the patient attempt to retrieve the offending memory simply by talking freely to a largely silent therapist. He also believed that unconscious needs expressed themselves in symbolic disguises that the analyst must decipher—the idea at work in his 1900 masterpiece, *The Interpretation of Dreams*. Freud's prestige may have waned, but the modern world is impossible to imagine without him.

DISCOMFORT ZONE *The couch on which patients reclined in Freud's office in Vienna, which has been restored at its original address as part of the Sigmund Freud Museum*

The Wright Brothers Find the Way to Make Workable Flying Machines

78 The dream of flight may be one of humanity's longest-held aspirations. The ancient Greeks imagined it in the story of Icarus, whose wax wings melted when he flew too close to the sun. A close student of bird flight, Leonardo da Vinci drew designs for artificial human wings made of cane, leather, and starched taffeta. In the 18th century hot-air balloons invented by the brothers Montgolfier in France launched people for the first time into the clouds. But balloons were playthings of the winds, subject to their movements. In the next century gliders, which gave the passenger-pilot more control, inspired much mechanical tinkering. In 1891 the American astronomer Samuel Langley even built an aircraft powered by a steam engine that sputtered along for just three-quarters of a mile.

It was the four-stroke internal-combustion engine, arrived at by the German inventor Nikolaus Otto in 1876, that made it truly possible to develop aircraft that could penetrate air currents and not just follow them. This spoke to a pair of scientifically minded bicycle-shop owners, the Wright brothers, Wilbur (1867–1912) and Orville (1871–1948). Neither had a high school diploma, but both had a long-standing fascination with machines. Inspired by the exploits of the German glider designer Otto Lilienthal, who died in the crash of one of his own gliders, they even built a wind tunnel to understand how their flying machine would perform in midair. Their great contribution was the invention of "three-axis control" achieved by means of a movable vertical tail fin. It gave the pilot the ability to master the plane's movement up and down and side to side, as well as its lateral roll. On Dec. 17, 1903, they were ready for Orville to launch himself across the sand dunes of Kitty Hawk, N.C. That first flight was brief—it lasted just 12 seconds and covered 120 feet. But in subsequent flights that day they increased the numbers to 59 seconds and 852 feet. Two years later an improved version of their plane, called *Flyer III*, was in the sky almost half an hour. For the record, there was no security check.

UP, UP, AND AWAY *Wilbur Wright on a glider flight at Kitty Hawk in 1902, one of many the brothers did before attempting engine-powered flight*

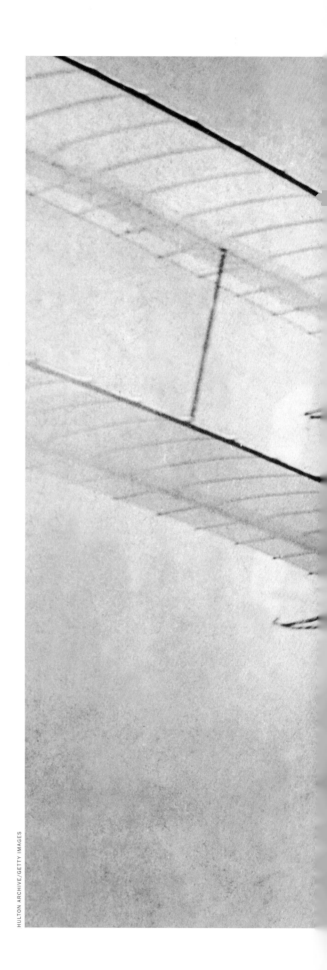

1ое
МАЯ
ВСЕРОССИЙСКИЙ
СУББОТНИК

№ 81

Lenin Produces a Ruthless Game Plan for Revolutionaries

79 Karl Marx expected that the first communist societies would emerge in the advanced industrial economies of Europe. He was wrong. It would be in Russia, a peasant society. This was due largely to the ruthless endeavors of Vladimir Ilyich Lenin (1870–1924). Trained as a lawyer, Lenin was exiled twice for revolutionary activities. During his years in England, Switzerland, and France he concluded that for a revolution to take place in Russia, a nation with no democratic traditions, it would be necessary for a revolutionary elite to lead the way. In his lengthy 1902 pamphlet *What Is to Be Done?* he argued that trade union activity, with its narrow focus on wages and working conditions, would never lead workers to an awareness of the need for sweeping political change. As a way to foster revolution he proposed a deliberately small and secret vanguard of professional revolutionaries who would politicize the workers and act on their behalf.

Lenin's critics objected that this vanguard would in effect substitute itself for the workers. That fear turned out to be well justified. In April 1917, with World War I dragging on, Lenin traveled in a closed railway car from Switzerland to St. Petersburg, then called Petrograd. He had been shipped east by the Germans in the hope that he would work to destabilize their Russian enemy. He more than delivered. In October the Bolsheviks, led by Lenin, seized power. Within a year all opposition parties were banned. The "revolutionary vanguard" would soon become the permanent dictatorship of the party elite.

REVOLUTIONARY ROAD *Above, Lenin speaking in Moscow's Red Square on the first anniversary of the Russian Revolution; at left, a Soviet poster promoting May Day, the international workers holiday*

Einstein Rocks the World With His Theory of Relativity

80 In a single miraculous year, 1905, Albert Einstein (1879–1955), who was then working in a patent office in Bern, Switzerland, published three scientific papers that utterly transformed science and the world. In the first, which would win him a Nobel Prize, he described the paradoxical behavior of light as both smoothly oscillating waves and discrete particles. In the next he laid out a way to confirm the existence of atoms and molecules, at the time still unproven. It was the third paper, on the special theory of relativity, that changed everything. It proposed that there's no such thing as "absolute" time or space. They are part of a single fabric, space-time, and they lengthen or contract depending on the motion of the person measuring them. That same paper contained the fateful equation $E = mc^2$, which says that energy equals mass times the speed of light squared. Though Einstein never intended it as a doomsday device, by asserting that matter and energy were different aspects of the same phenomenon and could be converted into each other, $E = mc^2$ opened the way to the production of atomic energy—and the atomic bomb.

Einstein would rock the world again in 1915 with his theory of general relativity, which extended special relativity to describe gravity as the bending of the space-time fabric. As with so much that he did, "mind bending" is the best way to describe it.

ALBERT EINSTEIN *Because of his immense impact on the world, in 1999, Time's editors selected him as Person of the Century*

BRAVE NEW WORLD *Picasso's 1905 canvas*
Les Desmoiselles d'Avignon — *a portrait of prostitutes*
at a brothel in Barcelona—is one of the pivotal images
of Cubism and modern art generally.

Modernism Explodes the Rules of Literature and the Arts

81 "Make it new" was the battle cry of the American poet Ezra Pound. It could just as well have been the motto of all the writers, painters, sculptors, composers, and architects we link in the very roomy category of "modernism." At some impossible-to-define point in the late 19th century, the arts in Europe and the Americas embarked upon a new age of formal experimentation and cultural provocation that represented a distinct break from the past. By the early decades of the 20th century the ferment was unmistakable in every department of culture. In literature there was the intricately structured fiction of James Joyce, Virginia Woolf, and Marcel Proust, the corrosive, fragmented poetry of Pound and T.S. Eliot, and the dream-logic plays of August Strindberg. Art produced the aggressively distorted space and form of Pablo Picasso and Henri Matisse, the anxious portraiture of Egon Schiele and Oskar Kokoschka, the ferocity of the German expressionists, and the pure abstraction of Wassily Kandinsky and Kasimir Malevich. In music there was the uncompromising dissonance of Igor Stravinsky and the atonality of Arnold Schoenberg, and in dance the unbridled movement of Vaslav Nijinsky and Isadora Duncan. In architecture one found the radically purified work of Le Corbusier and Ludwig Mies van der Rohe. Working in different realms, with different aesthetic problems to solve, all were making it new.

The cultural historian Peter Gay recently identified a unifying impulse across all the many types of modernism, something he called "the lure of heresy," the pleasure to be found in "the sheer act of successful insubordination against ruling authority." The irony, of course, is that by now those great acts of insubordination have been absorbed into the canons of great art. Modernism has become just one more tradition.

SQUARED CIRCLE *Mandalas like this one from 15th-century Tibet were images that fascinated Jung, who painted his own.*

Carl Jung Explores the Idea of the Collective Unconscious

82 One of Freud's most illustrious disciples, Carl Jung (1875–1961) was also one of the first to break with the master. Jung believed that the psyche was composed of three parts. Two of them, the ego and the personal unconscious, were accepted by Freud as well. But to those Jung added a third region he called the collective unconscious, a reservoir of psychic material common to all people consisting of, as he put it, "mythological motifs or primordial images."

Its basic structural unit is the archetype, an innate disposition to experience and understand life through one or another powerful symbol. So, Jung taught, the needs and expectations represented in the unconscious by the "mother archetype," needs we are born with, govern our relations not only with our actual mothers but also sometimes with mother figures in the outside world—a school, a church, even a forest or ocean. The son of a Protestant clergyman, Jung was fascinated by religious and mythic symbolism, including Eastern religions and mystical traditions of all kinds, which he believed express the content of the collective unconscious. His thinking has been particularly influential in the arts. The mythic themes of the Star Wars films, for one, owe much to George Lucas's reading of Joseph Campbell, whose work drew heavily on Jung. Jung's theory of personality types, such as the introvert and extrovert, also led to the development of personality profiles widely used by employers.

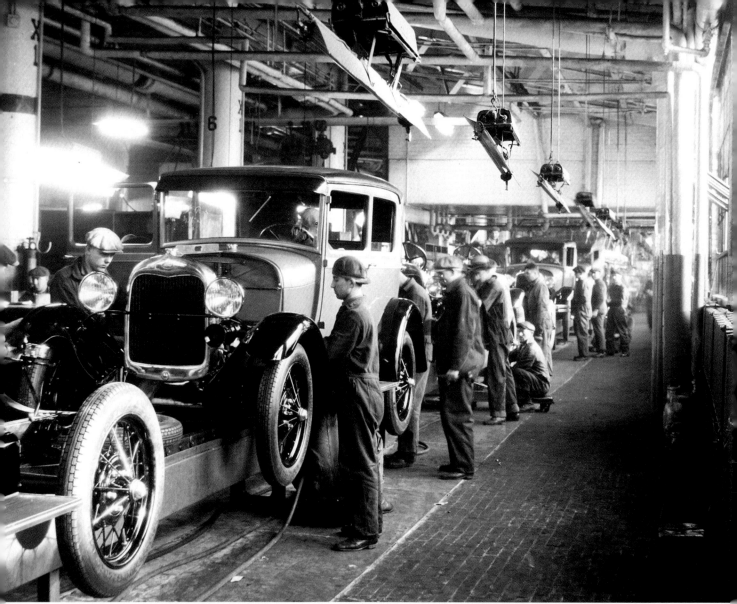

In 1928 workers at the Ford plant in Dearborn, Mich., put finishing touches on the Model A, the successor to the Model T.

Ford's Assembly Line Revs Up the Age of Mass Production

83 Henry Ford (1863–1947) was just one of many men, including the Germans Gottlieb Daimler and Wilhelm Maybach and the American Ransom E. Olds, who contributed over the years to the invention of the automobile. Yet however much cars revolutionized society, another idea more closely associated with Ford alone changed the world just as dramatically. In the first years of the 20th century automobiles were small-batch luxury items, individually assembled by teams of skilled workmen for the small number of buyers wealthy enough to afford fine craftsmanship. It was Ford's ambition to produce an automobile for the masses. To do that would require his engineers to perfect a method of manufacture—mass production—that would permit cars to be completed quickly and in large numbers.

The crucial element of the method was the assembly line. Instead of a worker going to the car to perform particular tasks, the car came down a moving line to the worker, who did the same job on each as it arrived before him. It was a technique employed as early as the 15th century at the Arsenal shipyard in Venice, where empty warships were towed down a central channel to be outfitted and equipped from stations on either side. In Ford's time, Swift meatpacking plants were using a similar system in the piece-by-piece disassembly of pig carcasses suspended from moving ceiling belts. But in 1913, at his plant in Highland Park, Mich., built expressly for the purpose, Ford unveiled an assembly line of unprecedented scale and complexity. For the next decade output would nearly double every year. In the same period, even with Ford paying his workers an unheard-of $5 a day, the price of a Model T dropped by two-thirds. The assembly line not only made his company for years the world's greatest, but provided a model countless industries would adopt.

Science Detects a Big Bang at the Beginning of Time

84 "This is the way the world ends," the poet T.S. Eliot wrote, "not with a bang but a whimper." Regardless of how the world ends, scientists tell us that the universe began with a bang. The Big Bang, as the theory is called, asserts that about 13.7 billion years ago the universe emerged from an infinitely small, hot, and dense point that astrophysicists call a "singularity." It began its expansion at once, soon producing a mass of particles like quarks and gluons. Those quickly combined to form protons and neutrons, and within three minutes the first atoms were emerging. (By this point temperatures had cooled to a manageable 1 billion degrees.) Next, the nuclei of hydrogen, the lightest element, began to appear in vast numbers, followed by other light elements. All this took just minutes, but it was another 380,000 years before the hydrogen gas cooled sufficiently to form molecules, and 200 million before the first stars coalesced. All the while, everything was rushing outward from that initial burst.

The Big Bang theory first began to take shape in calculations published in 1927 by Georges Lemaître, a Belgian priest and physics professor. Working with Einstein's theory of general relativity, Lemaître decided that the universe must have originated in a "cosmic egg" and was constantly expanding. At around the same time, the American astronomer Edwin Hubble discovered that every galaxy is moving away from our own, a sign that the universe is indeed expanding. And in 1965 two scientists working at Bell Labs in New Jersey stumbled upon the cosmic radiowave background, radiation left over from the Big Bang whose existence physicists had predicted. And how will the expanding universe end? Perhaps by contracting back into itself. That's called the Big Crunch.

KABOOM! *A computer-generated imagining of the universe continuing to expand as a result of the Big Bang*

The Surrealists Go Forth in Search of the Uncanny

85 Surrealism emerged from the tumult of Dada, the anarchic cultural movement that developed in Zurich, Berlin, and other cities in response to the calamity of World War I. As the artist Jean Arp, one of its founders, would write, "Dada wished to destroy the hoaxes of reason." By 1922, Dada had run its course, but some of its subversive energies were resurfacing in a new movement emerging in Paris. Its leader was Andre Breton, a onetime Dadaist who retained Dada's taste for chance as a creative tool and for art made without the guidance of rational faculties. Surrealism aimed to usher in an era of absolute freedom through contact with the liberating forces of the irrational. Its poets, critics, artists, and intellectuals exalted the power of the subconscious mind. To them, whatever was unnerving, uncanny, or fetishistic was a potential path to a beneficial new understanding of the world.

Though surrealism didn't begin as an artist's movement, it was through art that it would leave its most enduring traces, from the vividly conjured creatures and landscapes of Max Ernst to the fantastical semi-abstractions of Joan Miro, and Salvador Dali's paradoxically realistic pictures of impossible dreams. By the late 1930s the threat of Adolph Hitler had chased many of the French surrealists to New York, where their energies dispersed. But even now, when something strikes us as strange or uncanny, we call it "surreal."

John Maynard Keynes Makes Deficit Spending Respectable

86 Though it still has its critics, the idea that governments should use deficit spending as a means to correct economic declines is a familiar one these days. But at one time it was unthinkable, an affront to the belief that free markets functioned best when left entirely alone. The man who developed and spread the idea of government intervention as a tool of economic policy was the British economist John Maynard Keynes (1883–1946). Chosen as a young man to be a delegate to the Paris Peace Conference that followed World War I, he watched in dismay as the victorious allies imposed harsh war reparations on Germany. Back in England he wrote *The Economic Consequences of the Peace*, arguing that the reparations would keep Germany impoverished and unstable in a way that would in time theaten all of Europe—the very thing that happened. The book made him a celebrity and ensured that after World War II the victorious Allies would not repeat their earlier mistake.

His most important work, however, was *The General Theory of Employment, Interest, and Money*. Published in 1936 in the midst of the Great Depression, it posited that governments have to run deficits when the economy is slowing. That's because during slowdowns businesses reduce their investments, leading to fewer jobs, less consumption, and even less reason for business to invest. So government must step in to pump money into the economy. Keynes's thinking would eventually be adopted by many industrial nations, especially after World War II. Before his death he also designed two crucial postwar institutions—the World Bank and the International Monetary Fund. Though disputed by some, Keynesianism remains very much a force in the world.

THE GREAT DEPRESSION *A food line in Cleveland in 1938, two years after Keynes published his great work on correcting economic downturns*

Fascism Rears Its Ugly Head

87 For a few decades in the 20th century the lethal doctrines of fascism flourished across large parts of Europe, with the dictatorships in Italy, Nazi Germany, and then Spain as its principal regimes. Not so much a political philosophy as a mood, even a sort of social pathology, fascism could still be said to have intellectual sources, most of them in the 19th century. You hear an early note of fascist polemic in the sulfurous hatred of reason, progress, democratic self-rule, science—of the whole legacy of the Enlightenment—put forward by the arch-reactionary political thinker Joseph de Maistre, a man who wrote, "The whole earth, perpetually steeped in blood, is nothing but a vast altar upon which all that is living must be sacrificed without end." Romanticism's rediscovery of medieval folktales and traditions opened the way to fascism's mystical aggrandizement of racial bloodlines and the *Volk*. And 19th-century nationalism set the stage for fascism's ultranationalism, its glorification of the state, and its worship of military might as the expression of a nation's greatness. "War alone brings up to its highest tension all human energy," exclaimed Italy's fascist leader Benito Mussolini, who seized power in 1922. "[It] puts the stamp of nobility upon the peoples who have courage to meet it." Ranks of uniformed armed men also spoke to the fascist love of spectacle, culminating in the almost operatic tyranny of Adolf Hitler's Germany, with its crimson swastika banners and floodlit outdoor rallies.

A sense of national grievance was always useful in bringing fascism to power. Italy and Spain once led powerful empires but by the 20th century were at the margins of European affairs. Germany labored under the burden of heavy war reparations after its defeat in World War I. By promising national rebirth, the fascists appealed to sizable numbers within their own nations. With its contempt for human equality and democratic self-rule, fascism was the most dangerous idea of the 20th century, and the successful struggle to defeat it in World War II was the century's crucial event.

ON THE MARCH *During a Nazi Party Congress in September 1935, party members goose-step through the streets of Hamburg. Four years later Germany would invade Poland, and World War II would begin.*

CHILD'S PLAY *In 1926, John Logie Baird (above) used this odd device to transmit a low-resolution still image of a puppet's head.*

Television Emerges From the Work of Many Minds

88 Once cinema and radio had been developed, inventors chased a new communications grail: a medium that could broadcast both sound and pictures. So powerful was the vaporware's appeal that its name, television, was coined long before the medium was perfected. Many people share the credit for its creation, but three inventors stand out: John Logie Baird, a Scot; Philo T. Farnsworth, an American; and Vladimir Zworykin, a Russian American. Farnsworth claimed that he got the inspiration for his version of television as a farmboy in Idaho. Noting the straight rows of soil he created with his plow, he posited that if he could break images down into a series of lines arranged in gradations of black and white, he could transmit the lines through the air like radio waves. He called the machine he built to scan reality into such lines an image dissector; it was an electronic tube with a photoconductive plate. His receiver was based on the vacuum-tube oscilloscope invented by German scientist Karl Braun in 1897.

Baird chose to dissect his images mechanically, using a system of rapidly spinning disks perforated with tiny holes to scan an image and similar disks within a receiver to recompose it; the process yielded fuzzy images. An electronic model was clearly superior, and Zworykin, like Farnsworth, created an electronic version of video. His camera, the Iconoscope, proved inferior to Farnsworth's, while his receiver, a Kinescope, was superior. By the late 1930s TV was ready for its closeup, but the Depression and World War II delayed its wide debut. The medium exploded after the war, as TVs invaded living rooms everywhere, driving revolutions in entertainment, politics, journalism, and social behavior that are far from signing off.

A British Genius Hits Upon the Idea Behind Computing

89 If all Alan Turing (1912–54) had done was answer a vexing question in mathematical logic, few would remember him. But the method Turing used to show that certain propositions in a closed logical system could not be proved within that system had enormous consequences. For what this eccentric young Cambridge professor did was dream up an imaginary machine—a typewriter-like contraption capable somehow of scanning, or reading, instructions encoded on a tape. As the scanner moved from one square of the tape to the next—responding to the sequential commands and modifying its mechanical response if so ordered—the output of such a process, Turing demonstrated, could replicate logical human thought. The device in this mind experiment acquired a name: the Turing Machine. And so did another of Turing's insights. Since the instructions on the tape governed the behavior of the machine, by changing those instructions, one could induce the machine to perform other functions. Depending on the tape it scanned, the same machine could calculate numbers or play chess or do anything else of a similar nature. Hence his device acquired an even grander name: the Universal Turing Machine.

When Turing published his ideas in 1937, no one recognized that he had provided a blueprint for what would become the digital computer. During World War II, however, he helped build a computer-like device that broke the Nazi codes to U-boats in the North Atlantic. He might have gone on to great things in computer design. But in 1952 he was convicted of "gross indecency" for acknowledging his homosexuality, then a crime in England, and forcibly subjected to injections of female hormones intended to curb his sexual appetite. Two years later he committed suicide.

ELECTRONIC BRAIN *In 1948 employees at a Philadelphia telephone exchange work with an early computer that stored billing information.*

Existentialism Defines an Absurd Existence

90 In the years before and after World War II, a group of French and German thinkers produced a current of thought in philosophy and literature that became extraordinarily popular in the West. Existentialism held that we exist without purpose and only through experience find meaning. Therefore it's up to each of us to define for ourselves the meaning of our lives. Though one of the first and most systematic existentialist thinkers was German, Martin Heidegger, the philosophy's most compelling, intellectually glamorous, and public figures were French. Jean-Paul Sartre (1905–80) developed the outlines of existentialism in his lengthy treatise *Being and Nothingness,* in which he famously declared that "we are condemned to be free." He also dramatized that paradox in literary works like the novel *Nausea* and the play *No Exit.* In 1949 his frequent companion Simone de Beauvoir (1908–86) produced her brilliant analysis of the role and fate of women, *The Second Sex.*

But the most popular of the group was the saturnine Algerian-born writer Albert Camus (1913–60). In his essay "The Myth of Sisyphus," a meditation on the predicament of humans attempting to make sense of a senseless universe, he memorably expressed a central existentialist tenet: the absurd. Reflecting on the Greek figure of Sisyphus, who is condemned eternally to roll a rock up a hill only to have it roll down again, Camus tells us that by recognizing the absurdity of his situation, Sisyphus gains at least the dignity of forthright clarity. "We must imagine Sisyphus happy," Camus famously concludes, for "being aware of one's life, and to the maximum, is living, and to the maximum." Camus died in the most absurd way of all—a car crash.

WALK THIS WAY *Gandhi takes his daily stroll with members of his family and staff in May 1946, a month of crucial negotiations concerning India's independence, which would finally be achieved the following year.*

TEA FOR TWO *Existentialist writers and romantic partners Jean-Paul Sartre and Simone de Beauvoir*

Great Leaders Prove the Great Power of Nonviolence

91 It's a philosophy that could be said to date back to Christ's admonition to his followers to "turn the other cheek." But the philosophy of nonviolence saw its most dramatic application in two powerful episodes of 20th-century history. Mohandas Gandhi (1869–1948), leader of India's movement to gain independence from Great Britain, once said, "There are many causes I am prepared to die for, but none I am prepared to kill for." He first applied that philosophy to the independence struggle in the Non-Cooperation Movement, a campaign from 1920 to 1922 that rested on tactics like a consumer boycott of British-made goods and a call for Indians to withdraw from British institutions in India, including schools, courts, the civil service, and police forces. Gandhi called off the campaign after violent clashes between police and protesters led to deaths on both sides, making him fear that the movement was losing sight of its nonviolent principles. But he would later pursue other nonviolent campaigns that would result in Britain granting independence to India in 1947.

In the decade that followed, Dr. Martin Luther King Jr. (1929–68) applied Gandhi's methods to the struggle to win civil rights for African Americans. In the face of constant provocations, including beatings, shootings, and the bombing of a Birmingham church, King led a nonviolent campaign of boycotts and civil disobedience that bore fruit in the Civil Rights Act of 1964 and the Voting Rights Act of 1965. Like Gandhi, King would be assassinated. But the example of both men lives on as an inspiration to the world.

Atheism Develops a Following

92 We don't know just when atheism—the belief that there is no God—first emerged, but we already have evidence of it in ancient Greece. In the fifth century B.C. the Athenian philosopher Diagoras decided to argue publicly that the Greek gods did not exist. Not long after, he also decided it would be a good idea to leave town for good. Atheism was a position few Westerners would assume openly again until the 18th century, when a radical skepticism about God emerged among a number of intellectuals and scientists, though it could still be a costly position to take. In 1811, while he was a student at Oxford University, the English poet Percy Bysshe Shelley composed his tract "The Necessity of Atheism." It concluded that "the mind cannot believe the existence of a God." It also got him expelled. In the 1860s British biologist T.H. Huxley introduced the word "agnostic" to describe a less absolute stance—that there was no plausible evidence for God's existence, but also no way to prove that he did not exist.

Recently atheism has become much discussed in part because of two books. *The God Delusion* by British evolutionary biologist Richard Dawkins and *God Is Not Great* by British-born American writer Christopher Hitchens combined arguments against God's existence with what the authors saw as the pernicious effects that religion has had throughout the centuries. Both have become international bestsellers—proving, if nothing else, that atheism is no longer such a dangerous position to take.

Science Discovers "Chaos"

93 Chaos theory. That's quite a notion. Is it possible to have a theory about something so chaotic? It is, and in recent years it's become a major subspecialty of mathematics, with applications in many fields. In brief, it's the attempt to explain the fact that large and unpredictable outcomes will occur in systems that are highly sensitive to their initial conditions. What kind of systems? Weather systems, traffic patterns, population growth. What are initial conditions? All the circumstances that combine within a system at any moment of observation. For a weather system that might include air pressure, humidity, and wind speeds. The tiniest shifts can affect the behavior of all the others.

It was actually a weather scientist, Edward Lorenz, who first stumbled upon chaos. In 1961 Lorenz was running weather simulations through a computer. Deciding to repeat one of his number sequences but not wanting to start it from the beginning, he resumed it midway, then headed off for coffee. When he returned, expecting to find that the sequences had duplicated themselves, he was puzzled to discover utterly different outcomes. Then he realized that the second time he ran the numbers, he had rounded off the first of them by an infinitesimal fraction, a tiny change that produced hugely different results. In 1972, Lorenz delivered a paper on his findings titled "Does the flap of a butterfly's wings in Brazil set off a tornado in Texas?" Ever since, the "butterfly effect" has become a popular way of understanding the implications of chaos theory. Little things mean a lot.

IN A WHIRL *Above, a view of Hurricane Daniel in 2006. Chaos theory helps to explain why weather is hard to predict long term. Self-replicating "fractal" forms like the nautilus shell (right) are of interest to chaos mathematicians.*

Sexual Orientation Becomes the Basis for a Social Identity

94 Sex we have always had with us, including relations between members of the same sex. But in the late 19th and early 20th centuries something began to change in Western nations. Men and women who sought relationships with their own sex began to see that aspect of themselves as a defining personal characteristic, a social identity drawn from what we would now call their sexual orientation. One watershed involved the celebrated Irish poet and playwright Oscar Wilde. In 1895 he was convicted in London of "gross indecency" in a trial growing out of his relationship with Lord Alfred Douglas and other young men. The highly publicized trial made homosexuality much more widely visible, with the effect of making more homosexuals aware that there were others like themselves.

In the years that followed, more men and women began to identify themselves as homosexual. World War II marked another turning point, as military life introduced to one another multitudes of "gays," a term that would enter the language more widely after the war. In 1951 the Mattachine Society, the first American gay rights organization, was formed in Los Angeles. All of this culminated in New York City on June 28, 1969, when a police raid at the Stonewall Inn, a gay bar in Greenwich Village, set off two nights of rioting. That event signaled the start of the modern era of gay activism and the full emergence of sexuality as an identity.

A NEW KIND OF SELF-AWARENESS *In the 1980s, gay pride demonstrators march in New York City, where the 1969 Stonewall raid had set in motion the modern gay rights movement.*

Behaviorists Discover "Conditioning"

95 What monetarism was to Keynesianism in the field of economics (a complete alternative worldview) behaviorism was to Freudianism in the field of psychology. Where Freud developed a complex model of the mind that put a strong emphasis on the role of the unconscious, behaviorists insisted there was no such thing as an unconscious—or for that matter, a "mind" that could be distinguished from the physical brain. Behaviorism's central premise: Things that organisms do, including acting, thinking, and feeling, can be understood as behaviors, which can be changed through "conditioning."

One pioneer was Nobel Prize–winning Russian physiologist Ivan Pavlov (1849–1936), whose famous experiments with dogs began with the observation that they would salivate in the presence of food. By associating the arrival of the food with a sound such as a metronome, Pavlov discovered that he could cause the dogs to salivate by sounding the metronome, without actually bringing food. He called this a "conditioned reflex," meaning it was learned.

By far the most prominent American behaviorist was Harvard psychologist B.F. Skinner (1904–90). It was Skinner who conceived the idea of "operant conditioning," showing that behaviors could by changed by positive or negative reinforcements. He popularized his vision in the 1948 novel *Walden Two*, about an ideal community where people have been conditioned to adopt beneficial behaviors. And he worked, with varying success, to bring his methods into the real world, even building a "teaching machine" to apply conditioning techniques to the classroom. As he famously once said: "Give me a child and I'll shape him into anything."

REWARDING BEHAVIOR *In a Skinner experiment in 1950, a pigeon learns that pecking the correct light will result in the delivery of a food pellet.*

ON LOCATION *Levi-Strauss in the Amazon around 1936.*

Lévi-Strauss Discerns the "Structures" of Thought

96 French anthropologist Claude Lévi-Strauss (1908–2009) devoted his life to studying "primitive" tribes. In the end he transformed how we understand ourselves. He rejected the idea that the primitive mind is less subtle and capable than our own. Anthropology was ordinarily concerned with identifying particular habits of each culture it studied. As the primary architect of "structuralism," Lévi-Strauss looked across cultures at mythologies and cultural practices, such as eating habits and kinship systems, to find the universal structures behind them. He identified capabilities, like the ability to see things as symbols of other things, that linked all cultures.

Trained in philosophy, Lévi-Strauss migrated to anthropology and in the 1930s worked among tribes in the Brazilian rainforest. In 1955 he published *Tristes Tropiques*, a memoir of those years that was a huge literary success. But it was in *Structural Anthropology* from 1958, *The Savage Mind*, published four years later, and the multivolume *Mythologies*, that he put forward the main lines of his thinking. As British anthropologist Maurice Bloch summarized it, for Lévi-Strauss, the human brain in any culture "systematically processes organised, that is to say structured, units of information that combine and recombine to create models that sometimes explain the world we live in, sometimes suggest imaginary alternatives, and sometimes give tools with which to operate in it."

Monetarists Say Money Matters

97 By 1963 the economic theories of John Maynard Keynes, which argued for the validity of deficit spending by government as the best way to correct economic downturns, had become a new orthodoxy. Even Richard Nixon, a Republican President, could declare himself a "Keynesian." That year a book appeared that would challenge head-on the Keynesian approach to policymaking. *A Monetary History of the United States, 1867–1960*, by American economists Milton Friedman (1912–2006) and Anna Schwartz, argued that control of the money supply was the key to sustained prosperity. Friedman, who would win the Nobel Prize in Economics in 1976, argued that the amount of money being printed by central banks like the Federal Reserve in the U.S. and the Bank of England should grow at a fixed low rate, equivalent to the rate of real growth in the gross domestic product. Those banks should have no leeway to accelerate or slow that rate in response to developments in the economy like recessions. Excessive increases in the money supply, he warned, would inevitably bring on inflation, without in the long run producing higher employment. Central bankers should focus on price stability.

Just as Keynes' ideas were heretical when he first put them forward, Friedman's "monetarism" was not widely embraced in the 1960s, when Keynesian policies appeared to be ensuring steady growth with low unemployment and low inflation. But in the decade that followed, a combination of high unemployment with high inflation, a development Friedman had predicted, persuaded many policymakers to reconsider. In the late 1970s President Jimmy Carter chose as Federal Reserve chief Paul Volcker, who tightened the money supply and brought down inflation, though at the cost of a severe recession. In the 1980s Britain's Margaret Thatcher also embraced monetarist policies for a time, with similar results. But after the collapse of 2008, Keynesian deficit spending was once again a tool used by many governments.

WHEEL OF FORTUNE *At the Bureau of Engraving and Printing in Washington, D.C., stacks of one-dollar bills are readied for release.*

ANYBODY OUT THERE? *Some of the 350 radio telescope antennas in the Allen Telescope Array, a SETI project in Berkeley, Calif.*

Mankind Goes in Search of Extraterrestrial Life

98 How can extraterrestrial life, which would presumably be a "thing," be considered an idea? Because not until that thing is discovered will it be more than that. But as ideas go, it's a singularly compelling one, a proposal we offer ourselves in the hope we're not alone in the vastness of space, and one that has spawned major efforts to explore space in search of any signs.

The ancient Greeks were already speculating on the possibility of life on other planets. But the modern fascination with ETs owes more to pioneers of science fiction like H.G. Wells. In books like *War of the Worlds* from 1898 and *The First Men in the Moon* three years later, he imagined belligerent Martians and insect-like lunar creatures—a reminder that theoretical physicist Stephen Hawking might have been on to something when he warned that humans should think twice about reaching out to alien life forms. "If aliens visit us," he predicted, "the outcome would be much as when Columbus landed in America, which didn't turn out well for the native Americans."

But the possibility of contact makes the search irresistible. Many of NASA's numerous space probes have had as one of their purposes the search for signs of life, or at least for conditions, like water, that would support life. Since 1984 the SETI Institute (Search for Extra-Terrestrial Intelligence), based in Mountain View, Calif., has launched and coordinated search efforts of all kinds. And *Voyager I* and *II*, spacecraft traveling beyond the solar system, even carry disks with messages for aliens who might intercept them, including sounds and images of life on earth, spoken greetings, and samples of music. It was a project supervised by the late cosmologist Carl Sagan, who greatly popularized the idea of extraterrestrial life. Yet when an interviewer pressed Sagan for his "gut feeling" as to whether life existed elsewhere, he wouldn't take the bait. "I try not to think with my gut," he said. "Really, it's okay to reserve judgment until the evidence is in." Spoken like a true scientist.

FROM LEFT: DR. SETH SHOSTAK/PHOTO RESEARCHERS; DANIEL PEPPER/GETTY IMAGES

People Begin to Ask: Do Animal Have Rights?

99 "The greatness of a society and its moral progress can be judged by the way it treats its animals." The words are attributed to Mohandas Gandhi, but the sentiment is one that many people have entertained.

In the ancient world animals had a contradictory status. In Egypt certain species, especially cats, could be treated as earthly manifestations of the gods, while others might be used with no regard for humane practices. The Old Testament book of Genesis gives Adam "dominion over the fish of the sea, and over the fowl of the air, and over the cattle, and over all the earth, and over every creeping thing that creepeth upon the earth"—a wide-ranging authorization that appears to assign to humans complete ownership of all other creatures. This helps to explain why it was not until 1822 that the first animal-protection law was adopted, a bill to protect horses and cattle passed by the British Parliament. Two years later the Royal Society for Prevention of Cruelty to Animals was established. An American society was formed in 1866.

A new era of animal-rights thinking began with *Animal Liberation*, a 1975 book by Australian philosopher Peter Singer, who argues that people and animals have an equal interest in avoiding pain. Others have countered that with rights come duties, something animals cannot be expected to understand, much less satisfy. The debate goes on but has already affected attitudes toward factory farming and alternatives like "humane husbandry." Many supermarkets carry things like free-range chickens and eggs that were once hard to find.

CLOSE QUARTERS *At "factory farms" like this one in Missouri, animals are kept in constant confinement until they are ready to be slaughtered.*

127

THE BLOGOSPHERE *A computer-generated image represents linking relationships among thousands of "blogs"—Internet web logs.*

A Software Engineer Dreams Up the World Wide Web

100 It started in the Swiss Alps. The year was 1980. Tim Berners-Lee (b. 1955), a British software engineer working temporarily at CERN, the European Laboratory for Particle Physics, in Geneva, was fooling with a way to organize his far-flung notes. Building on ideas then current in software design, he fashioned a kind of "hypertext" notebook. Words in a document could be linked to other files on Berners-Lee's computer. But why not, he wondered, open up his document— and his computer—to everyone and allow them to link their stuff to his? So he cobbled together a coding system—HTML (HyperText Markup Language)—and designed an addressing scheme that gave each web page a unique location, or URL (Universal Resource Locator). And he hacked a set of rules that permitted these documents to be linked together on computers across the Internet — HTTP (HyperText Transfer Protocol).

And on the seventh day, Berners-Lee assembled the World Wide Web's first browser, which allowed users anywhere to view his creation on their computer screen. He alerted the world by way of a message posted to a newsgroup, and the world came. On Aug. 6, 1991, the web made its debut, instantly bringing order to the chaos that was cyberspace. From that moment on, the web and the Internet grew as one, often at exponential rates. Within five years, the number of Internet users jumped from 600,000 to 40 million. Until then, we hadn't really known what a powerful new tool the computer could be for everyone. Now we do.